MR. FROM BARKING

A FIRST SELECTION

TONY CLIFFORD & HERBERT HOPE LOCKWOOD

A personal history of Barking at the beginning of the 20th Century

2002

PREFACE

This is the first in a series of selections from a unique manuscript account of Barking written by William Holmes Frogley in the closing years of the 19th century and the early years of the 20th. The author was an ordinary person who compiled this work as a labour of love. Because of the importance of the content to local and family historians, as well as to the general reader, I am delighted to include the series in our ongoing and popular publications programme.

Bert Lockwood, the prominent local historian, has contributed an introductory essay to this book, which summarises his detective work into discovering the identity of the author and the history of the manuscript. I would especially like to thank Bert for allowing us to use his colour photographs of the illustrations in the manuscript, which are a credit to his photographic and computing skills.

Tony Clifford has been a major contributor to our publications programme, and in June 2001 received a Civic Recognition Award for his "outstanding contribution in publicising and promoting the heritage of the Borough". He has frequently used the Frogley manuscript as a source of information, and I know that the production of this series of books will give him the enormous personal satisfaction of making the content available to a wider audience. Tony has personally transcribed, edited and annotated all the text reproduced here, and is already at work on the second selection.

This is a time of great interest in local history and heritage, and our publications programme will continue to exploit and promote the rich collections maintained by the Libraries and Heritage Services in the Borough of Barking & Dagenham.

Trevor Brown
Head of Library Services
London Borough of Barking & Dagenham

Cover picture: the Fishing Smack, pre 1902.
(photograph loaned by Mrs Blyth of Upminster)

MR FROGLEY'S BARKING: A FIRST SELECTION

INTRODUCTION

Frogley's Place in Barking History

Although the following pages are only a selection from Frogley's 'History of Barking' yet they are a landmark in the manifestation of Barking's heritage.

For over three centuries the three most remarkable individual histories of Barking have all remained in manuscript. Each was a unique product of its time, though all were basically amateur efforts inspired by a sensitivity to heritage and locality. Smart Lethieullier's History was the work of an eighteenth century gentleman scholar and Lord of the Manor of Barking. Edward Sage was a middle-class professional land agent and Deputy Steward of the Manor when he compiled his History in the middle of the nineteenth century. But William Holmes Frogley was the son of a Barking fisherman who completed his history of this expanding town in the first decade of the twentieth.

Some of the content of Lethieullier's history found its way into print in Lyson's *Environs of London* but for a century the original was thought to have been destroyed by fire. Following its first exhibition to a meeting of the Essex Archaeological Society in 1863, few realised that Sage's Barking collection had later been deposited in Stoke Newington Library by his son. But the very existence, let alone the content, of the Frogley manuscript was generally unknown more than forty years after the death of its author.

More recently all three works have been reproduced in microfilm or photocopy; but the number of copies available has been limited by cost and restrictions on undue handling of the originals. Moreover these are handwritten documents of considerable length – the Frogley MS has nearly five hundred foolscap pages - which require manual transcription to put them into print. So financial considerations combined with the limited market for local publications have proved an even greater obstacle to their further appearance. In 1984 the Frogley MS itself was exhibited in Barking Central Library during the Golden Jubilee Exhibition of the Barking Historical Society and in 1993 the Essex Society agreed to loan it to Valence House Museum. This publication is a major step towards making Frogley accessible to all.

Further, this particular Selection exhibits Frogley's peculiar ability for taking us by the arm on a personally conducted tour of the streets of Barking at the

MR FROGLEY'S BARKING: A FIRST SELECTION

turn of the nineteenth century. Not only are we shown the buildings with summaries of their history but given a candid introduction to hundreds of residents and their antecedents. In short this is more than a history, it is an illustrated guidebook to Victorian Barking and a gossip column about our ancestors. Yet if we turn to look at our guide we find his face hidden in shadow.

For both the manuscript and its author remain something of an enigma. In those five hundred pages he reveals only a little of himself. It has taken years of research to establish his first names and even now some lingering doubts remain concerning his identity. We are still puzzled as to how he learnt so much about others without calling more attention to himself.

The Discovery of the Manuscript and Search for the Author

The manuscript was discovered – or more accurately, rediscovered – in 1965. Dr Emmison, the Essex Archivist, came across it when he happened to be working in the library of the Essex Archaeological Society in Hollytrees House in Colchester. It was indexed under the name of Frederick Brand, an old Barking antiquarian who died at Ilford in 1939. Brand was well known for his excellent 'Essex Bibliography' as well as a number of shorter works – written, duplicated and bound by his own hand! But it now appeared that Brand had also written a full scale History of Barking without ever revealing the fact.

Characteristically Emmison immediately informed those whom he thought might be particularly interested in his unexpected find. They included Ray Powell, editor of the newly completed volume 5 of the Victoria County History of Essex, and the late John Gerard O'Leary, secretary of V.C.H. Essex and contributor of the Dagenham section, and also myself who had done some of the work on Barking and Ilford. O'Leary, still Chief Librarian of Dagenham, though about to hand over to the newly created London Borough of Barking, instantly ordered a Xerox copy to be made and bound for local use, although the discovery was just too late to assist with the new volume of V.C.H.

Then came a further surprise. The work was without a title page or the signature of an author and Dr Emmison, delving deeper, had now found the vital passage at the foot of p.312 where the writer quietly reveals himself to have been the son of a Barking fishing captain called Joseph Frogley. So the

MR FROGLEY'S BARKING: A FIRST SELECTION

cover of the Valence Xerox had to be hastily retooled with the name Frogley in place of Brand.

Subsequently I found that the Index compiled by Brand to his own library around the mid-1930s (surviving in the Brand Collection purchased by Ilford Library after his death) contained an entry, "A MS History of the Town of Barking with rough sketches said to be by the late Mr Frogley" which seemed to put the matter of authorship beyond doubt. And in the *Transactions of the Essex Archaeological Society* for 1939, their librarian had reported under 'Accessions' that "An illustrated MS History of Barking the gift of the late Mr F.J. Brand is also worthy of mention." No doubt the outbreak of World War 2 and the death of Brand in December 1939 could account for the inadequate cataloguing and virtual disappearance of the volume.

Yet problems remained. How had Fred Brand acquired the manuscript in the first place? The wording of his catalogue entry suggests that he had no direct contact with the author before the latter's death. I had several conversations on the subject with the late Dr James Oxley, the only living person to have been shown the manuscript by Fred Brand. As far as James Oxley could recollect, Brand indicated that it had been bought from someone in need of ready money and seemed reluctant to allow Oxley to examine it for himself. This was uncharacteristic of Fred who was notably generous to his friends - amongst whom the young Oxley was certainly included.

One can only speculate on the reason. It must have come as a shock to Fred Brand that someone could have written such a work on Barking without Brand being previously aware of it. For William Holmes Frogley was of his own generation (Brand was born in 1857) with a similar background (Brand was the son of a North Street grocer and a mother who came from a Barking family of ship's chandlers and sailmakers); and William Holmes had spent his childhood in the same quarter of Barking and developed parallel interests to Brand. Was Fred Brand contemplating editing and publishing the manuscript himself before age and a Second World War overtook him? Or another work on Barking in his own name incorporating some of the material?

Nor did the entry on p.312 completely identify the author since external evidence soon showed that Joseph Frogley had four sons. The eldest, Joseph Arthur, could be immediately eliminated since he died in 1904, well before the work was completed. But internal evidence gave no direct help in choosing between the other three – for instance not one illustration was

5

initialled. Several passages however seemed to point towards the second son, William Holmes Frogley, whose death in 1924 also fitted well enough with Brand's purchase of the manuscript and catalogue entry. Further evidence was required before his two younger brothers, Frederick William and Charles Albert, (particularly the former), could be finally eliminated. This only became possible quite recently with the acquisition of their death certificates which proved that Charles Albert had died in Barking in 1940 and Frederick William in Plaistow in 1941 – so neither could have been referred to by Brand's index as 'the late Mr Frogley'.

The Identity of the Author.

William Holmes Frogley was born in Barking in the first quarter of 1855, son of Joseph Frogley, one of Hewett's sea captains (who had begun as apprentice to Samuel Hewett in March, 1834!). This Joseph Frogley was the 4th generation of Barking fishermen with that name. The one who was also landlord of 'The Blue Anchor' in 1814, whom William Holmes names as his ancestor on p.394, was the 2nd generation and so the great-grandfather of the author. Jane, mother of the author, was the daughter of a builder called William Holmes after whom he was named. On p.352 he expresses great admiration for his uncle, James Holmes, landlord of the 'The George Inn'. His ancestry and many connections with well established Barking families were no doubt initial reasons for his interest in Barking history as well as a source of information.

The 1861 Census shows the mother and the boys living in Manor Road; Charles Albert was only a baby of 10 months and their father was at sea. We can only guess where William Holmes was sent to school; it is possible that, like Fred Brand, he went to a private school in nearby North Street, but it is more probable that he attended the Church National Society School, the history of which he recounts at length. But by the 1871 Census the 15-year-old had already become a grocer's apprentice, and the limitations of his formal education probably account for the peculiarities of his grammar and sentence structure. Incidentally, he was then living in Ivy Cottage, Queens Road, which was next to the Swan beerhouse (alias Laurel Cottage) and so illustrated on p.473. His father still describes himself as a 'Mariner'; but the Barking fisheries were now in terminal decline and it must have been around this time that he sought fresh employment in building (p.495). He later

MR FROGLEY'S BARKING: A FIRST SELECTION

became a factory storekeeper.

By 1881 we find William and his brother, Frederick, running a grocery together in the Plaistow Market in Beckton Road. In 1884 he married Eliza Jane Crockford at West Ham and the following year their daughter, Gertrude Jane, was born. By 1888 he had his own grocery business at 1 Market Place, Gypsy Lane (Green Street), Upton. Possibly this venture foundered because in the 1891 Census he and his young family were living with his wife's sister and her husband at 5 Station Road, Plaistow, and he is described as an 'insurance agent'.

During the 1890s he appears to have moved into the business of an estate agent with premises in Vicarage Lane, Stratford. He may have been working again with Frederick Walter because he too became an estate agent in the area. Both brothers also became certified bailiffs. They may even have found employment for the youngest brother, Charles Albert, who had become a carpenter. There is need for further research here as elsewhere because it was during the period between the late 1890s and 1910 that the history seems to have been written. The internal evidence suggests that William Holmes was especially active in the Barking area around 1906 (see pp.425, 477 & 480, 453). Did a thriving business give him leisure for study and the occupations of house agent and certified bailiff make it easier for him to make enquiries and sketches without arousing much comment from fellow citizens or the media?

Family affairs must also have often drawn him back to Barking during the period. His father's fortunes had been improved by a legacy following the death in 1883 of a sister, Mary Anne Earle, a shipwright's widow "well provided for" (p.377), and he moved to a new house, Windsor Cottage, 44 Longbridge Road. Joseph died there in 1902 at the age of 82; his wife, William Holmes' mother, had died the year before. The eldest son, Joseph Arthur, a factory engineer who never married, continued to live there until he died intestate in 1904. William Holmes was administrator of his estate and, presumably, a major beneficiary. Both his younger brothers had married in 1893 but only Charles, who had (literally) married the girl next door, finally settled in Barking.

The internal evidence from the manuscript suggests that William was actively writing down to 1910 but it looks as if his visits were becoming less frequent or his enthusiasm was waning. There are a couple of notes added as late as 1913. One refers to the site of Barking Abbey yet, curiously, the

7

MR FROGLEY'S BARKING: A FIRST SELECTION

author seems oblivious of Clapham's well-publicised excavations early in 1911, which aroused much local interest. What caused William Holmes Frogley to lose his interest in a project to which he had devoted so much attention and effort over a period of years?

We know so little about the author's remaining life that we cannot answer the question with any confidence. Yet the answer may lie in the few facts that we do know. By 1918 he was already living at 108 Henniker Gardens, East Ham with wife, daughter and son-in-law, George Capel. Here he died on 22 May, 1924 and according to his death certificate he had reverted to his old trade of Grocer and Provision Merchant. Perhaps the change of occupation and lifestyle had already occurred by 1911. Certainly by that date the phenomenal suburban expansion of West Ham and even of East Ham had slowed down reducing opportunities for house and estate agents – and William Holmes was now 56 years of age. But the rest is speculation.

His widow, Eliza Jane, continued to reside with the Capels in East Ham until her sudden death on the 20th May 1935 at the Monteagle off-licence, Fanshawe Avenue, Barking which was kept by Edwin William Barnett, a relative and former neighbour of the Frogley family. There is some evidence to suggest that she had been working in the area as a nursemaid or a part-time housekeeper.

Perhaps it was she who arranged for the sale of the manuscript to Fred Brand who was now widely known as a local historian. For public interest in the history of Barking had been stimulated by the Pageant of 1931, by the publication of several books, and by the formation of the Barking and District Historical Society in 1934. Old Mrs Frogley may have realised for the first time that her late husband's papers might have a monetary value. We don't know how much Brand paid, but in his catalogue he valued it at £1. 10s. He certainly bound it himself.

MR FROGLEY'S BARKING: A FIRST SELECTION

Structure and Sources.

Although this is an Introduction only to a section of the document it is as well for a proper understanding that the reader should be aware of the general plan of Mr Frogley's History This is perhaps all the more important since this part is, very approximately, the last quarter of the whole.

For someone who – so far as we know – had had no formal instruction in the subject his plan was well conceived. Only the main 'chapter headings' can be given here – a full Contents List with page numbers is to be found in the Essex Record Office Catalogue T/A 333/1 which can be easily accessed via their SEAX website.

The Introduction is followed by an account of Barking Abbey, followed by St Margaret's Church (including clergy, churchyard, and charities). Then an 'illuminated' title page introduces The Manor of Barking, which is a section of almost 80 pages covering estates and manor houses. Another lengthy chapter follows on Local Government which includes past elections and schools, amongst other topics. Frogley is enlightening on local political contests – a subject often neglected by local historians. The next section on Churches in Barking (other than the parish church dealt with above) contains facts which could usefully have been included in volume 5 of the V.C.H. had the manuscript surfaced earlier. The chapters that follow cover what we should term, Economic History, viz. agriculture, fishing (included in the present Selection) and other industries.

Next comes the long section on the Streets of Barking, much of which is covered by the extracts in this publication. But this first Selection deliberately omits Frogley's more detailed coverage of certain topics such as the Market House and National Schools (which it is hoped will figure in a future production). Finally there are shorter chapters on Creekmouth (also included here), Beckton and Dagenham Gulf, concluding with one on Embanking.

Unsurprisingly there are digressions from the strict order. Right at the beginning of the History, his Introduction wanders off into an account of the Forest of Waltham, which ends up with Daniel Day and Fairlop Fair before beginning on Barking Abbey. And as we follow him up the Church Path to the Curfew Tower we are unexpectedly treated to a dissertation on the "Origins of the Church of England together with the various Religious bodies now established in Barking" before he conducts us into St Margaret's.

MR FROGLEY'S BARKING: A FIRST SELECTION

We notice instances even in the present Selection when, to take only one example, a 1688 token for the Ship Inn triggers an explanatory footnote on Essex trade tokens (p.296). However Frogley may be didactic but he is too full of curious detail and human interest to become boring. Moreover one feels that he has taken a lot of trouble to discover the facts and having taught himself is anxious to help others in the quest for knowledge. Indeed Frogley is almost a model of 'self-help' on the Samuel Smiles' pattern.

His curiosity about people and things and his considerable powers of observation and enquiry are matched by a width of reading, which largely compensates for the apparent shortcomings in his basic education. The East of London Family History Society are at present finalising a project to construct an Index to the whole Frogley manuscript. In the course of this they have attempted to list the sources used by Frogley – not a simple task since he seldom gives detailed references – even so, the range is surprising.

It shows that Frogley was familiar with all the standard 'county' histories such as Lyson's Environs of London and Morant's History of Essex as well, as those by Cox, Muilman, Norden, Ogbourne, Salmon and Wright. He also made considerable use of Stow's classical Survey of London as well as now lesser-known volumes like Hughson's *London: The British Metropolis and its Neighbourhood*. Moreover he looked at works published at his time of writing such as the first volumes of the Victoria County History of Essex and recent numbers of periodicals like The Essex Review. Amongst contemporary local historians, he was obviously well acquainted with Edward Tuck's *A Sketch of Ancient Barking Its Abbey and Ilford* (the work does not bear comparison with his own) and noticed Shawcross' work on Dagenham and Tasker's on Ilford. Whether he knew any of them personally is doubtful; they never appear to have noticed Frogley!

It is also plain that Frogley had access to the older general histories and reference works such as Rapin's *History of England,* Dugdale's *Monasticon,* and Newcourt's *Repertorium*. In addition he quotes occasionally from a wide variety of specialised books such as Fisher's *History of the Forest* and Ivimey's *History of the Baptists*. Sometimes his quotations are not exact – but photocopying had not yet been invented and he may not have had the time or inclination to make full notes. In any case Frogley makes few academic pretensions but his facts are generally accurate enough. One has to assume that he was his own tutor; and sometimes he shows notably sound

MR FROGLEY'S BARKING: A FIRST SELECTION

judgement in distinguishing between conflicting authorities.

But where did he find such a range of printed source material in one library? It is highly unlikely that the Barking 'free' library of the time could have supplied his needs. Perhaps future research may show that the rapidly expanding municipal collections of West and East Ham were adequate at the period. But present information would seem to point to the Guildhall Library in the City of London, or even the British Library.

Locally Frogley seems to have made a good deal of use of committee minutes (such as those of the Vestry, the School Board and Burial Board) and sometimes of back numbers of the *Essex Times*. But I am puzzled by his long list of monuments in St Margaret's Churchyard since I am under the impression that the official survey by the Barking U.D.C. was not until 1930 – yet it seems unlikely that Frogley created his own list. Exceptionally, his account of the origins of the Dove House Estate appears to have depended on primary source material – probably property deeds. It is difficult to know to what extent these various sources were supplemented orally.

Incidentally the Index to the whole MS mentioned above, which is being published in microfiche by the East of London Family History Society, also gives some indication of the potential value to researchers of the ultimate publication of the complete manuscript. It includes over 3000 personal names and nearly 1400 minor place names – a veritable goldmine for the family or local historian.

The Illustrations

As described in Fred Brand's Library Index the manuscript was illustrated by 'rough sketches'. That is indeed how Frogley himself referred to some of them; and Brand, who was himself an amateur artist with a penchant for impressionism, readily accepted the description. But the illustrations in the following pages should enable readers to judge for themselves.

The early Xerox copies certainly could not do them justice. So in 1979, Jim Howson, then Curator of Valence House, borrowed the manuscript from the Essex Society (its first return to Barking) and assisted by Rob Gehringer and my son, Richard, we spent almost a week taking colour slides. Flattening sufficiently whilst protecting the binding presented a problem, which was not

MR FROGLEY'S BARKING: A FIRST SELECTION

completely soluble in the case of the large 'double-page spreads' sometimes favoured by Frogley. Modern computer technology has enabled me to 'enhance' these images for the present publication and to largely eliminate the 'guttering'. However, I, not the Editor, must accept the blame for any distortion or misrepresentation introduced into the originals even by such well-intentioned manipulation.

I hope that the reader may agree that many were somewhat better than 'rough sketches'. As Frogley explains, several were executed hurriedly when an old building was under imminent threat of final destruction. In certain instances, as in the case of the ancient 'Blue Anchor' tavern, Frogley has provided us with the only illustration in existence; in others, the only pictures in colour. He does not himself seem to have possessed a camera; but sometimes a parallel photograph of similar age enables us to judge the accuracy of his representation. His sketches appear to score well in such a test despite certain problems with perspective and drawing from life. On the whole they could be described as a valuable supplement to William Holmes Frogley's text and an attractive addition to Barking's heritage.

Herbert Hope Lockwood
September, 2001

MR FROGLEY'S BARKING: A FIRST SELECTION

Notes on transcription.

The family of the author of this manuscript lived in Barking for at least five generations and were related to many local tradesmen. William Holmes Frogley (1855-1924) - we are now certain of the author's identity - was clearly educated to a reasonable standard. Although not written or illustrated with professional polish, this account of Barking from the mid 1890s to just before the First World War accurately records its subject matter. This is confirmed in the footnotes, which are intended to match up the author's descriptions with other contemporary records, such as commercial directories of Essex (which at that time included Barking). The author takes us on a conducted tour of Barking, describing many buildings which have now disappeared. He shows us glimpses of the past and introduces us to the inhabitants of the town. It is a wonderful example of one man's obsession with recording the history of his native town.

The handwriting in the manuscript is generally neat and easy to read, although tiny on occasion. To put investigations on a more scientific basis, we need to find other material written by William Holmes Frogley to compare with this manuscript. We also need the opinion of a handwriting expert to confirm whether the manuscript is the work of a single person, or several.

Throughout this narrative I have tried to retain the author's original spelling and grammar, to preserve the historical context and the spirit of the narrative. Faced with the option of changing whatever was necessary to suit contemporary usage and vocabulary, I originally decided to apply a few simple insertions to make the text more approachable to the modern reader, whilst preserving the content of the author's manuscript. On later reflection, this made the text too complicated to read, and I soon abandoned this approach.

There are consistent mistakes in the use of grammar; for example, the use of "was" as a plural instead of "were", and virtually no use of apostrophes. Extremely long sentences and paragraphs are often stringed together by using "&"s, hyphens and other punctuation, which causes havoc with modern electronic grammar checkers, the use of which I more or less gave up on.

Square brackets – [ ] – have been used whenever any query or alteration of the original text has been required. For example, there are sometimes gaps in the text where a word or date has been omitted, for whatever reason, and I have indicated this with "[ ]". I have used round brackets – ( ) – whenever

MR FROGLEY'S BARKING: A FIRST SELECTION

the author has used them in the text; they also indicate the insertion of a relevant footnote from the original manuscript into the appropriate point in the text. Very rarely, I have missed out text because of repetition, duplication, irrelevancy, or because it will be included in a future booklet in this series; this is indicated by "…".

Interjections and asides are frequent in the manuscript, and the concluding comma or hyphen of the inserted text is often omitted by the author. I have inserted the missing punctuation for ease of reading. There is frequent use of "&c" in lists, the equivalent of the modern "etc". This sometimes develops into "&c &c" or even "&c &c &c".

Frogley makes frequent use of capital letters in nouns. Perhaps some extra emphasis or importance is intended with regard to certain trades, professions and activities by giving them a leading capital letter. "Auction" is a typical example, and perhaps gives a clue as to how he may have obtained some of the information in the book. In particular, any trade connected with the fishing industry usually has a capital letter, and he clearly has a great affection for this part of Barking's history, in which his family was involved for many generations. He was clearly not in favour of any of the "improvements" inflicted on the town by the railway, and usually prefixes any account of them with "so-called".

I have drawn heavily from this manuscript in my own books and articles, and it has been a real pleasure carrying out the transcription and research for this book. I am delighted that the contents will now be available to a wider audience. I have spent a lot of time thinking about how the author must have organised himself to produce such a relatively neat manuscript, with very few corrections. This first selection from the Frogley manuscript concentrates on the fishing industry, the Town Quay, and the town centre as it was around 1900, before the epicentre shifted towards the railway station and expanded to the north and east.

Tony Clifford

MR FROGLEY'S BARKING: A FIRST SELECTION

North-Street. [Pages 321-370]

This is the principal street in the Town and is undoubtedly so named from its northerly direction from the Church. It extends from the "George Inn" to Tanner Street, although some 50 years back a portion of it, viz, from the George Inn to the Barking Road was known as High Street. Starting from Tanner Street and passing a few residences is Dangerfields Cottages, and opposite a Beer-house called the "Jolly Fisherman". The name reminds us of the time when there was a great many Jolly Fishermen in Barking, and the same remark could be said of their wives also. When David Argent[1] was landlord he also carried on the building trades there, but he unfortunately failed in 1894, but he resided in the house after for many years. In November 1906 Mr Jones was landlord, and he in that year transferred it to Mr Kitson[2], who pulled down the old house and rebuilt the present structure.

Dangerfield Cottages [Page 327]

These cottages were evidently built by one of the Dangerfield family[3]. They are opposite the "Jolly Fisherman" beerhouse in North Street. The Dangerfields was an old family of Barking Parish. James Dangerfield died in 1846 and his wife Sarah in 1837[4] – both are buried in Barking Churchyard. Also in 1740 William Dangerfield – an ancestor – was a Churchwarden at East-Ham, and was the Landlord of the Rising Sun, Ilford. Henry Dangerfield probably built these cottages and he owned land near to them. He died in 1839 leaving a daughter, who died without issue).

Cowbridge Lane – nearly opposite – leads to the marshes. On page [ ] is a view of this Lane in 1900, and also a plan of the piece of land attached to the houses in the lane. This piece of land contains about [1.5] acres. In 1823, Henry Taylor died possessed of it, and it later was owned by Henry Dangerfield who died in 1839. His property then went to his daughter who

---

1   David Argent, builder & grocer, Wakering Road. (Kelly's 1874), beer retailer & builder, North Street. (Kelly's 1886, 1890).

2   Walter John Kitson was at the Britannia, Church Road, in 1890.

3   A family of local builders. "On 5 July 1832, John Dangerfield was asked to submit proposals for building cottages on the north side of the Market Place". Oxley, J.E. *Barking vestry minutes*, p.129. Henry Dangerfield, builder, High Street & James Dangerfield, builder, Ilford. (Pigot 1839); they are also listed as carpenters & undertakers.

4   *St Margaret's churchyard: register of graves*. 1930.

MR FROGLEY'S BARKING: A FIRST SELECTION

died without issue. Edmund Hugh Mundy[5] next possessed it. In 1887 it was offered for auction sale, but not sold. I am told that there is a query respecting the title, and if so, there are this day the same doubt respecting other pieces of land in the town. The Friends meeting house and burial ground is described on page [ ].

Braintree House[6]

This apparently old bricked & tiled house stands in its own grounds on the corner of Kings Road.

Union Terrace and Union Street [Page 322]

(made up, sewered & kerbed in 1889 at a cost of £200) - the former built in 1826, these small houses were occupied by a respectable class of fishermen, but Union Street has for many years been occupied by a very inferior class. At one corner is a general shop and was for many years kept by a Mr Knowles, making apparently sufficiently to allow him to retire in his old age. On the other corner is a greengrocers, but formerly a beer-house "The Duke of Wellington", formerly a cottage. The tenant for many years was a Charles Willsmore[7], who however was more popular as a Violinist. He, and a companion known as "Blind Scotcher" – a Harpist – was well known at the dancing booths when Barking Fair existed. Also up to recent years these two practically constituted the Christmas Waits [8]. In 1875 Mr Willsmore sold the Beerhouse business for £40 to Mr James Scotcher – a fishmonger of East Street[9] – who purchased it for his brother the "Blind Harpist". The latter died in 1890 and soon after James Scotcher sold it again to Messrs Inde Coope & Co the Romford Brewers, as a surrender in favor of the Burford Arms, Stratford Bridge. The price he received was £150. Mr Willsmore was alive in 1907 and gained an existence by his violin.

---

5   Edmund Hugh Mundy, beer retailer, 59 Fisher Street. (Kelly's 1890).
6   John Willett, Braintree House. (Kelly's 1890). Churchwarden 1873-78 & 1882-84. *Barking vestry minutes*, p.326.
7   Charles Robert Willsmore, beer retailer, North Street. (Kelly's 1874). Charles Willsmore, age 49, musician and Louisa Willsmore, age 36, wife. 1881 census, Gorleston.
8   Waits – "A band of musicians and singers who perambulate the streets by night at the approach of Christmas and the New Year playing and singing carols and other seasonal music for gratuities". *Oxford English dictionary*: vol.19. 2nd edition, 1989.
9   James Scotcher, fishmonger, 69 East Street. (Kelly's 1890); fishmonger, The Walk. (Kelly's1894); fishmonger, 1 Cobham Road. (Kelly's 1900).

Moffatt. James, Manager to Cleas.t Hewett. His wife Mary Ann died in 1892.

Quash. John. of Northbury House, Brackbournes. Originally a Fisherman after a Captain suddenly became possessed through a relation of some thousands of pounds. He purchased Brackbury House & where his descendants still live. His wife Mary pre-deceased him 1900.

Harvey. George. Mr Harvey of 1 Jersey R.d Lynn. Age 62 - son of Robert Harvey &c owner of considerable property in Barking & Lynn & retired from the Fishing Business of Cleas.t Hewett & Co at Corleston. The wife of Mr R. Harvey George was a daughter of the late Robert Hewett. He owns the Ringfield Estate Lynd.

Frogley. Joseph. retired Fisherman. For 34 years Captain of an Cleas.t Hewett's Steam Trawler & the revised Catholic in his house "Windsor Cottage" Longhope Road — now the property of the Railway Company. His wife Jane daughter of the late William Holmes of 206 L.t Barking died 96 — she respected Parents of the writer. They were interred in the Cemetery.

The passage at the foot of page 312 where the author's identity is made clear. (See pages 4 and 99).

THE JOLLY FISHERMAN PH 1907

Pages 328 - 329 in the manuscript (see page 15).

Daagerfield Cottages. 1900

These Cottages were evidently inhabited by one of the Dangerfield family. They are called the "Jolly Fishermen" Seahorses on Roath St. The Dangerfields were an old family of Barking Beach. James Dangerfield died in 1846 and his wife Sarah 1837 — both buried in Barking Churchyard. Also in 1750 William Dangerfield — an ancestor — was a Churchwarden at East Ham, and he was the Landlord of the Rising Sun, Ilford. Henry Dangerfield probably built these cottages and he owned land near them. He died in 1831 leaving a daughter, who died without issue.

Page 327 in the manuscript. (See page 15)

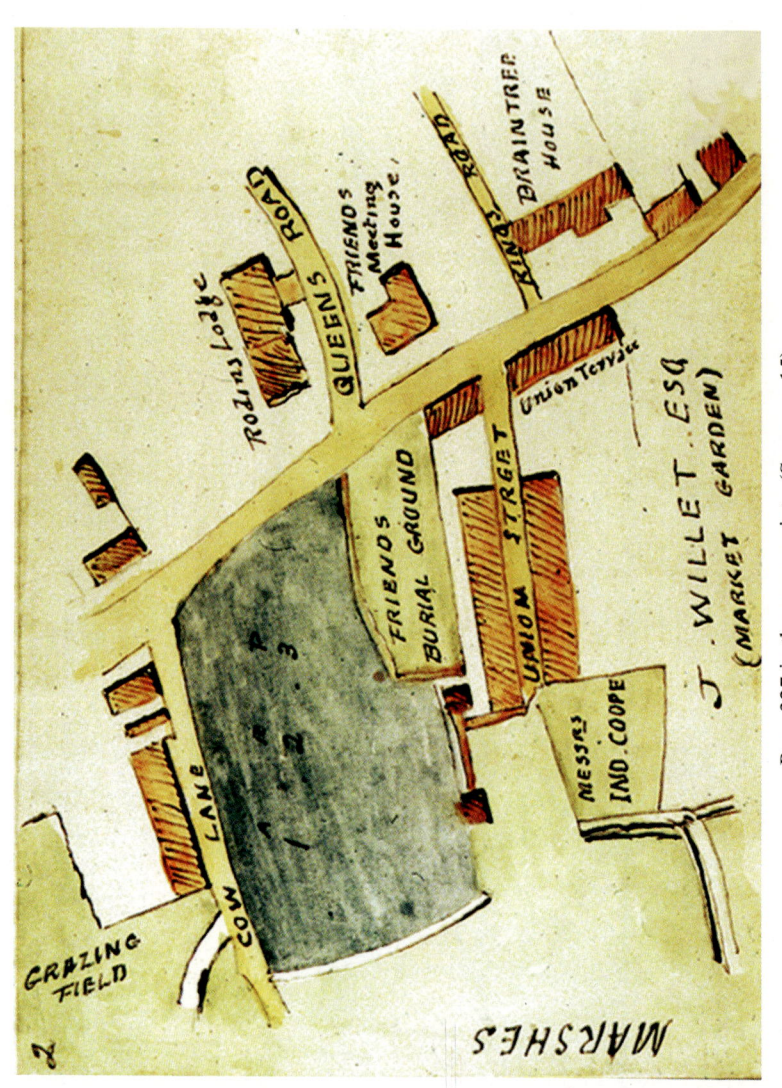

Page 327 in the manuscript. (See page 15)

Union Terrace. 1900. Built 1826.

This terrace built in 1826 was afterwards the residence of Captain of the fishing smacks. The shop in the right hand corner was the "Duke of Wellington" Beer house — now a Greengrocers. (La Inne)

Page 330 in the manuscript. (See page 16)

BLIND SCOTCHER THE HARPIST

Page 322 in the manuscript. (See page 16)

The eldest Sunaway brother. Page 323 in the manuscript. (See page 25)

John Graham of the Bull. (See page 34)

MR FROGLEY'S BARKING: A FIRST SELECTION

Braintree Terrace – five small houses – built on the site of some very old wooden houses, mostly occupied by a family – relatives – named Sunaway[10]. They were all costermongers or Street Hawkers of fish &c.

The Good Intent [Page 323]

– a beerhouse. When a private house, it was occupied by a Market Gardener named Samuel Baxter who later lived in a cottage opposite. His successor – Mr Spinks – about 1850 obtained the Licence, being assisted by Mr Watkins[11] Sexton of the Parish Church, and a Watch and Clock maker. After obtaining the Licence these two friends were considering the sign of the house, when Mr Watkins in his remarks said "Well Spinks I have assisted you with a good intent":- "Ah", said Spinks in stopping him in his remarks, "We will call it "The Good Intent" ". Previously to the present alterations the house was entered by a door in the centre – up some steps.

Opposite the Good Intent is a new house, occupied by the Leftley family – carriers[12]. This business was for many years the livlihood of Mr John Jaggers. He resided in East Street and his van collected parcels from and to London daily. On the site of this new house was an old cottage, occupied for many years by a Mr Wall, who had a smith and farriers business attached. After his death the family left the town, and Mr Charles Leftly took the place later as "Carriers"; but the sons has extended the buisness as cartage contractors.

St Johns Retreat, [Page 324]

consists of several cottages built about 1880. This site was previous to 1880 a piece of land with three cottages in the rear of it, and in one resided a Mr Caustin, who had a saw pit on this land. (The antiquity of these hand saw pits is astonishing. The first saw mills introduced into London was erected in 1663 by a Dutchman, but he was compelled to abandon it on account of the fury of

---

10 Family grave of James and Susan Sunaway in *St Margaret's churchyard: register of graves*. James Sunnaway, Fisher Street and John Sunnaway, Heath Street are among the 61 Barking smack owners listed in Pigot's 1839 directory and the 76 in White's 1848 directory. They are not listed among the 27 in White's 1863 directory.

11 Probably the Watkins listed as Parish Clerk in 1853. *Barking vestry minutes*, p.326.

12 James Leftley, carrier, High Street. (Pigot 1839, White 1848). Charles Leftley & Son, carriers, 22 Nelson Street; Mrs Isabel Leftley, carman, 86 North Street. (Kelly's 1890, 1894, 1900).

the mob. It was not before 1767 that another was erected by a Mr John Houghton of Limehouse, and it was driven by wind. A jealous mob however demolished this, but the third one was not interfered with (Smiles[13])). There was several of these saw pits in the town, but machinery & other causes have abolished them. This spot however is more historical from the fact that a "Mansion" originally stood here[14]. In the 18th century there was several of these large houses in the Town, but I cannot locate them all.

Reform Place [Page 324]

– consists of 10 houses, and some at the back called Back Reform Place. They were built in [ ] by Mr William Holmes of Axe Street[15], Barking. (He also built the local Gas Works and Loxford Hall). The shop, formerly a cottage, was opened in 1866 by a Mr Stapleton as a butchers, whose father was well known as a member of the "Baptists". This site – including the Police Station - is where Barking Jaol stood for centuries and often contained Smugglers, Poachers, Body-snatchers, Quakers &c. An old inhabitant described it to me as a large building surrounded by a high brick wall, and in or annexed to the wall was a shop, occupied by Mr Wallis, a boot and shoe repairer. This jail was built in 1790 on the site of an older one demolished, and its style was Gothic, having solitary cells and working rooms. Early in the 19th century, the Governor was Mr Thomas Miller and he died in 1815. In December of 1815 – at Chelmsford Quarter Sessions – his son was elected to succeed him. He – the son – at that time kept the shoemakers shop already mentioned, and Wallis as a lad was apprenticed to him, and eventually took over the shop. The Prison was demolished in 1834 and the prisoners taken to the new jail at Ilford.

(Ilford Jail [Page 325]

was erected in 1831 at a cost of £30,000, but was later enlarged. It was

13 Samuel Smiles (1812-1904), prolific author and social reformer. It is not clear at the moment from which of his books Frogley obtained this information.

14 A conveyance of 7 Sept 1877 of a piece of land and 4 cottages in North Street from E. T. Camplin to J. Sivell (now in the Valence Museum archive) shows this was the site of the White Hind. This house, presumably a tavern, is mentioned in other documents, including the 1609 manorial survey (PRO LR 2/214, fo.245). So Frogley was not so far out.

15 William Holmes, bricklayer, Axe Street. (Pigot 1839). Elizabeth Garbett (d.1891) was a daughter of Jeremiah Holmes of Axe Street, "and aunt to the author" – section relating to St Margaret's churchyard.

MR FROGLEY'S BARKING: A FIRST SELECTION

surrounded by a strong stone wall and moat over which was a drawbridge. It occupied the site of the present Worcester and Gloucester Roads, and extended from the Romford Road to the Railway. There are to-day (1908) a few large stones having the broad arrow on them still laying carelessly near the path in the Romford Road. They were a part of the jail. The Governor – Mr John Anderson - died in 1852 & his wife in 1879).

Mr Wallis told me that the prisoners here had little to complain of, and it was common to see a prisoner holding the head of the Parsons horse in the roadway, whereas now it would require some-one to hold a prisoner if once outside its walls. Mr Wallis carried on the boot repairing business in the cottage opposite the "Good Intent"[16], but getting old he was in 1889 appointed caretaker of the Free Library at 14/- weekly, with house & firing. In 1895, on account of his age, he was allowed to resign on a small allowance. He died 1899. Aged 82.

The *Police Station*. [Page 325]

Barking is in the district of the Metropolitan Police, of which Ilford forms a sub division – K – and includes Barking, Dagenham & Chadwell. In 1898 there was 1 Sub-Divisional Inspector, 1 Sub-Ditto, 6 Station-Serjeants, 12 Serjeants, and 87 Constables. The Police Station in North Street was built in 1842. An old inhabitant says that previous to the introduction of the "Police force" in 1840 to Barking, the town contained only two of the old police and that "Vine Cottage" in Tanner Street was the Station.

Particular Baptists [Page 332]

– this body meets in a house adjoining the Police Station, which previous to them taking it in [ ] was occupied and used by Mr Woodard, as a private school[17].

The Red Lion – this sign supposed to be "Heraldic" also figures on our Royal

---

16 William Wallis, boot & shoe maker, 92 North Street. (Kelly's 1886).

17 "From about 1862 there was a Baptist mission room in North Street, presumably as a branch of Queen's Road; this continued until about 1908. In 1909 members of the Tabernacle started a mission in Heath Street, which was later transferred to Abbey Road, as the Abbey Hall Mission, and subsequently to Gascoigne Road as Emmanuel Mission". VCH Essex, v.5, p.245). Fred Brand was a pupil at Mr Woodward's Academy for Young Gentlemen – see his *Barking in 1866 and all what* (1937), p.10.

MR FROGLEY'S BARKING: A FIRST SELECTION

Arms, and is painted in all colours. The Bosworth family[18] have had this house for generations. The old house stood more on to the path. It had one small entrance, and the bar was really a room, and the counter which was small had a glass casement above it – similar to so many of the Inns about the country. It had a projected sign, with a red-ramping Lion painted on each side. In 1899 it was pulled down, and the present handsome fabric erected at a cost – I am told – of about £10,000. Also at this time George Street was continued to North Street, by cutting through the well kept garden at the rear of the old house.

George Street is a new street, and in the making of which Mr George Bosworth, of the Red Lion, was summoned for having made the road less than 40 feet wide. But as the Clerk of the Local Board ommited to give a written notice signifying dissaproval of the plans submitted to the Board and other reasons the case was dismissed on Section 158 of the Public Health Act 1875, and the summary jurisdiction Act of 1888.

Northbury House, the residence of Mr John Quash Junior. This old house was originally the old Vicarage, but some portions of it is modernised[19]. A family named "Reed" resided here; they were smackowners, and Mr John Quash Senior became possessed of it next. Mr Quash was a fisherman, but was fortunate in having a large sum of money left to him and he also had some vessels. He died in 1902 and is buried in the Churchyard. For a further account of this family see "Churchyard"[20].

The White Horse. [Page 333]

This is not an old licence – probably dating back to about 1850. As a private house it was in 1830 tenanted by William Holmes, builder, and later it was a butchers. It is a beer-house and in 1850 John Henry Goodaker[21] took it and probably obtained the Licence. He also had here a Wheelwrights business –

---

18   Mrs Susannah Bosworth, Red Lion, North Street. (Kelly's 1874); George Bosworth, Red Lion P.H., North Street. (Kelly's 1890).
19   Frogley does not explain how he arrived at this certainty of Northbury House being the old vicarage. For an explanation by Herbert Lockwood read *The Barking vicarages and Jeremy Bentham* in *Essex journal,* Summer 1992, p.43-47. "After having been the home of the Quash family, it became the Northbrook Club, before it was demolished around 1937 when the London Road was extended through to meet the Ripple Road".
20   Frogley's section on St Margaret's churchyard will be included in the next book in this series.
21   John Henry Goodaker, beer retailer, 59 North Street. (Kelly's 1886, 1890, 1894).

MR FROGLEY'S BARKING: A FIRST SELECTION

he having learned the trade from his father who had a business in 1845 in Axe Street. After 45 years he sold the beerhouse to William Langman (1895) of Upton Park. Mr W. Langman purchased other small beer-houses in Barking, with the idea – it was said – of surrendering them if he was successful in obtaining a full licence for the "White Horse", but being refused he disposed in 1896 of all these houses. Mr Goodaker still continued his other business, and he died at 20 Barking Road on 8th October 1905 and is buried in the Cemetery at Rippleside.

No [ ] North Street is a small hairdressers. One tenant – Mr Walter Cotton[22] - kept it for 40 years and retired in 1906, dying the following June (1907), Age 63.

No [ ] North Street was a private school kept by a Miss Pegram, but she married a successful tradesman and the school was dissolved. (Miss Pegram married Mr Edward Harris – she was his second wife. He came to Barking in 1857 and commenced business as a Farrier in the Broadway[23]. He has two sons, Edward a Chemist, & Frederick a Blacksmith at Rainham. He was an expert quoit player and for many years the Captain of the Barking Club[24], and became an Amateur Champion. Some of his prizes are very valuable. A Dr McDonald of Barking presented him with two prizes:- one a silver sheild; and a solid gold quoit for his success in winning several matches. He was a man well respected by all. In 1878 he married Miss Elizbeth Pegram, and building a nice villa – now called Myrtle Villa – in North Street, he with his new bride went to live there. He died on 7th February 1906, Age 74). Here is the old National School (see School board).

Nelson and Trafalgar Streets almost suggest when they were made. Every house no doubt was at one time occupied by fishermen.

The Workhouse buildings. [Pages 335-338] The large plain brick edifice was erected under the powers of an Act of Parliament, obtained in 1786 and they were completed in 1787. The site they occupy previously contained a Mr Rayments Brewhouse & Malthouse, and an old school building – called

---

22 Walter Cotton, hair dresser, 38 North Street. (Kelly's 1890).
23 Edward Harris, farrier & smith, 41 Broadway. (Kelly's 1886); blacksmith. (Kelly's 1894).
24 Barking Quoit and Skittle Club: club house and grounds, the Peto Arms; captain, E. Harris; treasurer, J.M. Tracey; secretary, E. Harris, jun. (*Essex almanac for 1889*).

MR FROGLEY'S BARKING: A FIRST SELECTION

Campbells Charity School[25]. The above Act vested the control of the poor in certain persons called "Directors" and under whom was four Guardians, who were elected annually – one in each ward. (Guardians were under this Act appointed for the first time). They had the immediate management of the poor in the Workhouse. The original Directors of Barking were The Revd Peter Rashleigh, Vicar; Mr Bamber Gascoyne, Senior of Byfrons; Mr Bamber Gascoyne, Junior of Byfrons; George Spurrell, farmer, of Roding Lodge; Thomas Pittman, farmer, of Loxford Hall; Edward Hulse, Lord of the Manor.

Under this Act the Directors were to be only those who resided in the Parish valued at £200 per Annum, or possessing a real estate for life in the Parish of the clear annual value of £100. They had the disposal of all the money collected from rates, except such as was disbursed by the Overseers of each Ward for casual relief (Lysons[26]). The frontage of the buildings to North Street was 140 feet and contained apartments for the Master and Matron: Committee room: Storerooms: and two wings on the ground floor – in the rear – contained long rooms for the looms. (Spinning and sack making was carried on there, and other trades. In 1831 a committee from the East-Ham Vestry visited this place to see the general working of it, and this is their Report: "We have inspected the poor house of Barking Parish and were perfectly satisfied with the good order and industrious habits introduced therein, which confirms our opinions, that farming the poor on the same principle for East Ham is the best to be adopted").

Above these was the bedchambers. The whole formed a square with piazzas supported by plain pillars for the recreation of the inmates after their labours. On the front was a large inscription in latin implying "This house of industry was built at the sole expenses of the Inhabitants of Barking to provide for, and protect the industrious – to punish the idle and the wicked &c". The cost of the ground, Building, and furniture was £5000 (Hughson[27]).

In 1796 there was 112 inmates in this Workhouse (Lysons). According to Mr Lester – an old inhabitant - the inmates was treated in a more humane manner than those in these days, and being in their native town, they was allowed to

---

25   In 1642 Sir James Cambell of Clayhall left money to found a free school in Barking.
26   Daniel Lysons *The environs of London.* T. Cadell, 1796.
27   David Hughson (pseudonym of David Pugh) *London: being an accurate history and description of the British Metropolis and its neighbourhood to thirty miles extent, from an actual perambulation.* 6 vols. 1805-1809.

MR FROGLEY'S BARKING: A FIRST SELECTION

visit their friends very often. But a new Act – the Union Act of 1837 - abolished local workhouses. Several parishes were united in the Romford Union, and at that town a new Workhouse was built in 1838 and the inmates here was transferred to Romford. The Gentry of Barking – I believe before the inmates were removed – and in consequence of the Coronation or wedding day of our late Queen, gave a substantial dinner and held a great demonstration in the Workhouse, and the inhabitants of the town were invited to attend. The Workhouse buildings was then leased to Mr Withers, Builder of Ilford for a term of 99 years, and at a yearly rental of £120. In the rear he erected several cottages and the front portion was converted into shops and I believe the following six gentlemen was the first tradesmen who had these shops:-

1. Mr John Willett, who commenced business here in 1844 as a Draper, but ultimately became a Pawnbroker & Auctioneer. In later years he resided at Braintree House[28] and in his last days became very feeble and helpless. He died in 1883 and his son Robert[29] succeeded him, and is a successful tradesman in the town. He closed up the Pawnbrokers shop in 1906 – transfering the business to the corner of Trafalgar Street. He has both corners, and they were two old schools.
2. Mr Pearson,[30] Butcher, an old inhabitant. He transferred his business to a shop in the Broadway & that is where he died. His son succeeded and he also is now dead.
3. Mr Brand,[31] Shoemaker – also a lay preacher of the Wesleyans for 40 years. He died in this business place in February 1895. His son is now living in Grange Road, Plaistow, 1900.
4. Mr Bolton, Grocer. Of him I have not any particulars.
5. Mr Brown, Beer retailer (see "The King Harry").
6. Mr Ford, Grocer. He came from Aylesbury to Barking in 1842. He had several children, of whom a daughter married Mr Charles Dawson, Surveyor of Barking Local Board. Also Walter Ford, who married a Miss Mills of Loxford Hall. Mr Ford, I was informed, married a Miss Holden,

---

28 John Willett, Braintree House, North Street. (Kelly's 1890).
29 Robert Willett, hosier & glover, 4 Broadway; linen draper & clothier, Broadway. (Kelly's 1890).
30 John Pearson, butcher, Broadway. (Pigot 1839). Three Pearsons, butchers, are listed in Kelly's 1890: Edward (60 North Street), James (39 Broadway), Robert (23 Heath Street).
31 David Brand, boot maker, 30 North Street. (Kelly's 1890). Richard Brand was a leather cutter & seller in North Street in 1839.

MR FROGLEY'S BARKING: A FIRST SELECTION

who was in his employ as secretary.

6. Mr Withers, son of the original Leaseholder, and who succeeded his father in the builders business, built the Catholic Church at Barking, but he retired from active business many years ago, and went to reside at Southend. In stature he was tall and had a commanding appearance. He visited Barking every week to collect his rents. He died at Southend in December 1897 and was buried there at St Johns Church.

Before leaving the Workhouse account there is one interesting matter I must refer too. It was a suggestion of Mr Samuel Glenny in 1891. In March of that year, the Romford guardians decided to spend about £20,000 upon the Workhouse at Romford. Now Mr Glennys sensible suggestion was as follows:

"That as Barking pays one-third of the whole rates of the Union and yet has not been consulted about this proposal – and East-Ham also complains about inadequate representation on the West-Ham-Board; would it not therefore be better to form a new Union – say of East-Ham, Barking and Ilford, and build a new poor-house in the neighbourhood, which would be a boon for those who unfortunately apply for relief and also for the Guardians themselves. The rateable value and population of the three Parishes are greatly in excess of very many existing Unions".

The Cooperative Stores [Pages 338-339] is now a branch of the Stratford Society[32]. There have been several attempts to establish a local Cooperative Stores in Barking, so long ago as about 1868, but for want of good management on business methods each attempt proved to be a failure. In 1889 another attempt was made and being supported by the Stratford Society it succeeded. Their shop was No 10 North Street – formerly an Hosiers and Hatters kept by John Quash Junior of Northbury House[33] – and it was opened in October 1889. It was called the Industrial Cooperative Society and the Shares £1 each. They in August 1890 took also the next shop - a milliners, called the "Bonnet Box" – belonging to the Misses Read[34], who leaving the town sold off all the effects by Auction. In the latter part of 1900 these two shops and the present buildings were erected on their site. The following particulars will shew their progress in a year.

---

32 The "beehive" crest of the Stratford Co-operative Society can still be seen over the shop at no.10 North Street. *Barking and Dagenham buildings past and present*, p.62.

33 John James Quash, hosier & glover, 10 North Street. (Kelly's 1886).

34 Mrs Sophia Reed, milliner, 8 North Street. (Kelly's 1886).

MR FROGLEY'S BARKING: A FIRST SELECTION

The King Harry – beerhouse – originally kept by a Mr Brown. In 1870 a Mr Webster kept it, who previously drove the Small Mail Cart from Barking to Ilford – since dispensed with. This cart was similar to the small Butchers carts, only painted red. Webster was there in 1888. The house was entered by steps but in 1901 it was altered and a large bar made. It closed up in 1907-8.

Years sales of the Cooperative ending March 1891 = £862. No of members 179. Years sales ending March 1892 = £1132. No of members 214. Years sales ending March 1893 = £1245. Years sales ending March 1894 = £1256. Members increasing.

The parent Society at Stratford originated in 1860 with 47 members and a capital of £27 and the sales effected the first year was £453 and the following shews their progress interesting.

Sales during year 1860 = £453. Members 47. Grocery only. Sales during year 1870 = £10334. Members 439. Various. Sales during year 1880 = £63997. Members 2007. Various. Sales during year 1887 = £90000. Members 3406. Various.

In 1887 their [Stratford's] Share Capital was £46,620 and during the existence of the Society – 27 years – they have paid £108,000 to its members in dividends.

Mr Bissells[35], Ironmonger &c. Mr J. Bissell Senior was a native of Evesham in Wiltshire, and came to Barking about 1850 as manager to Messrs Mabbets & Pinks, Ironmongers on the Broadway. He opened the shop near the Bull, and afterwards greatly associated himself with the Church and Parochial affairs. He died in 1892 and was buried in the Churchyard. Subsequently his son removed the business to the opposite side of the road.

The Bull. [Pages 339-340]

According to a recent clipping, this house and some old houses adjoining in East Street is the property of the United Westminster Schools, and the Clerk of that body writing in 1907 to the Board of Education explained how it came into their possession. In 1636 – three years after Charles I granted a Charter of Incorporation to St Margarets Hospital, London - the governers purchased the above property for the nominal sum of one-shilling. The Title Deeds date

---

35 John Bissell, Ironmonger, 6 North Street. (Kelly's 1874, 1890); Barnett & Bissell, ironmongers, 6 North Street. (Kelly's 1894). John Bissell, Churchwarden, 1888. *Barking vestry minutes*, p.318.

MR FROGLEY'S BARKING: A FIRST SELECTION

back to 1435 and commence with a lease dated in that year – under its present name – and there appears to have been some ownership connection with the Abbey. The house, known to the writer, was a dull, heavy building, of brick faced with rough mortar or cement and projecting from the angle of the house was the primitive sign of a Black Bull reposing – as if at rest – on a platform. The size of the figure I should say was about 6 feet long or life size. During the year 1885 it was much altered – in fact nearly rebuilt – but the old heavy appearance was retained. The house was in the possession of the "Parsons" family for over a century – a Mrs Parsons, Widow, carried on the business until her death in 1850 and her son George succeeded, and he died in 1883. He was well known as a strong advocate of the "Tories", and his party frequently held their meetings at his house. His son George[36] succeeded him, and he married his servant – a tall and prepossessing young woman named Fitch, daughter of Mr Fitch the local dustman. Mr Parsons, retiring from business in 1899 sold it to a Mr W. A. Medcalf of Canning Town, formerly a butcher, but he the following year sold it to Mr J. Graham.

The Graham family previously had the Abbey Arms, Canning Town. Mr George Graham, of the Abbey Arms, was a champion Quoit player, and was well known at Barking. I am informed that he has retired from business for many years, and now enjoys a very quiet life in his residence at Chadwell Heath. During the time Mr Graham had the Abbey Arms it was a low, old fashioned country Inn, with stables and sheds adjoining. In the rear was a running track, and other sports was carried on there. It is a singular fact, that although Barking possessed such a renowned Abbey, there is no "Abbey-Arms" in the town, nor has any of the Inns a sign reminding us of the famous Monastic Buildings.

Lake and Kings [Page 341]

– Drapers &c. From here, viz from East Street to Axe Street, was the part originally known as High Street, but now it is locally called the "Broadway". This shop was formerly a small shoemakers shop, tenanted by Mr John Lake, who was also the last liveried "Beadle" of the Church. In his time the choir sang from a gallery at the west end of the church, and under the gallery sat boys and girls – divided – and a cosy seat for Mr Lake. He died in 1873 and his son William succeeded[37]. At the formation of the local board in 1882 he

---

36 Kelly's lists Joseph Parsons in 1886 and 1894.
37 William Lake, house agent & collector to local board, East Street. (Kelly's 1886); 30 Longbridge Road. (Kelly's 1894).

MR FROGLEY'S BARKING: A FIRST SELECTION

was appointed Rate Collector, and held it up to his death in 1895. Mr Lake, his brother, in partnership with Mr W. King of Barking, had the premises altered and opened the Drapery business there.

Next door is a grocers many years back held by Mr Harris. The shop parlour in his day had shutters – trellist kind – painted green. Mr Grainger[38] later had it for many years. He died in [ ]. Also his second son James, died during his tenancy of the Leonards Arms, Wennington, Essex. His widow now carries it on.

The Chemists, for many years possessed by Edward Fitt, and who was able to get a competency out of it. He died in 1880, and was succeeded by his son Frank Fitt, and after great success he sold the Freehold and Business in 1888 to Mr Thomas Pelling for £1100, and Mr Fitt, who had married a daughter of Mr Pearson Butcher of the town, removed to Deal in Kent and opened a Chemists shop there. In 1888 the business at Barking was sold to a Mr C. Ridley and he died there in 1906. His wife succeeded in the business and also was allowed to fill his place as a Guardian.

The Drapers – 50 years ago, and later, was carried on by Mr F. D. Harwood[39]. He sold the business to Mr Robert Willett[40] – of whom more will be said on another page. Mr Harwood died in 1898 at Leighton Buzzard. Passing the Congregational church is some large shops, built in recent years. They are built on the site of four smaller shops, of which I have drawn a view as seen on page [ ]. The four shops was occupied by the following tradesmen in the writers time:-

Mr Rose [Page 342] had the shop adjoining the chapel as a Grocers. It laid back from the path, which was narrow, and had an iron fence in front. He had a son – a lovely singer – and a favorite in the Church Choir, but as a boy he died of consumption. After Mr Rose, a Mr Maine had it, and he was there a few years. Afterwards Samuel Sutton[41] took it and altered it into a greengrocers. (Edward Sutton previously carried on a small business in a shed at the corner of Church Path and North Street). He [Samuel] was the last tenant.

---

38 William Grainger, grocer, Broadway. (Kelly's 1886).
39 "The family grave of F. D. & J. Harwood" gives the date of death of "F-D-H" as 9th December, 1866. *St Margaret's churchyard: register of graves*.1930. p.218.
40 Robert Willett, clothier 2, hosier & glover 4, & linen draper 7 Broadway; pawnbroker 22, 24 & 26, & house furnisher 32 & 32a North Street. (Kelly's 1900).
41 Samuel Sutton, pork butcher, Bamford Place, Wakering Road & Mrs Eleanor Sutton, fruiterer, Broadway. (Kelly's 1886).

MR FROGLEY'S BARKING: A FIRST SELECTION

Fergusson (Mr Fergussons shop originally was the private room of the Grocers shop which had a door in the centre and on one side a parlour and shop the other. When Mr Sutton took it as a greengrocers he altered it in this way). Shoe shop – Mr Fergusson[42] is not a native here, but his family came here many years ago. He is still there in the new shop. His brother married a Miss Wade of the Barge Aground[43].

Reed. Tobacconist. Mr George Reed[44] was also an assistant at Messrs Mabbets & Pinks, Ironmongers, Barking[45], but through a great trouble – entirely his own fault – it so disturbed his mind that he committed suicide.

Harts – Butchers. Mr Legasicke originally had this, but he sold it to Mr Fergusson – an elder brother of the two mentioned above – and later Mr Joseph Hart[46], son of Mr Hart, Butcher, East Street, purchased it and is now in the new buildings. These old shops – relics of Barking – was demolished in 1890 to make room for the noble shops now standing. The Contract price for the Building of Mr J Pellings – the Grocers – was £1852 and of Mr J. Harts £894.

Mr Thomas Pelling, Grocer &c, came into Barking and opened a shop on the opposite side of the road in 1874 with his brother. He did not appear to have been so successful until he married a daughter of Mr Edward Deveson[47]. He is now a man of property in the town as will be seen. His private residence is Fawley House in East Street – which will be noticed later.

Mr J. Moffatt, [Page 347] manager to Messrs Hewett & Co, resided in a double fronted house adjoining these old shops. (Mr James Moffatt was a corpulent man and by his workmen was considered a "bully". He died suddenly while on a visit to Margate in 1881. His widow later removed to her house "Farm Villa", Longbridge Road, Barking; having been left in a position to enable her to lead a retired life. She died in March 1892, and her property and

---

42 Henry Fergusson, boot maker, 11 Broadway. (Kelly's 1900). See "The great boot robbery" in H. H. Lockwood, *Barking 100 years ago*. 1990. p.44-46.
43 William Foster Wade, beer retailer, Broadway. (Kelly's 1894).
44 George Reeds, tobacconist, Broadway. (Kelly's 1886).
45 John Thomas Pink, ironmonger, 43 Broadway. (Kelly's 1886, 1894).
46 Joseph Hart, pork butcher, Broadway. (Kelly's 1886); butcher, 15 Broadway. (Kelly's 1894).
47 Edward Deveson, Victoria Terrace, Fisher Street. (Kelly's 1874); Edward Deveson, corn & coal merchant, Broadway & Fisher Street. (Kelly's 1886).

MR FROGLEY'S BARKING: A FIRST SELECTION

effects was sold by Auction shortly after by Mr Samuel Glenny, and this was the first Auction Sale by him in Barking). It [the house] was set a short distance from the pathway and had an iron fence in front. It was built of brick and was not an old building. In 1876 it was sold with three old sheds adjoining (not the 3 mentioned above) by Auction & Mr Lake – of Messrs Lake and Kings - purchased this property with other land in the rear – the houses & shop were pulled down and the present shops erected on the site, but an idea can be had of the demolished shop as one shop was not touched, being occupied by:-

Thomas Forge[48] – Newsagent, Watch and clock repairer &c. Mr Forge came from an old Barking family who owned Smacks[49]. This Thomas Forge was son of Richard Forge who died in 1861, a Smackowner. Thomas commenced business in this old shop in 1842 as Watch and Clock maker and he continued so for 40 years. He also added the newsagency & stationery business, and was the first local agent for the Essex Times, which started in 1862. He was also one of the first members of the "Foresters" society in Barking and which started here in 1851 and became their Secretary[50] : Overseer to the Parish: Clerk to the old "Lighting and Watch Committee" that ceased to exist in 1881 and Captain of the Fire brigade – if it was worth that name. He had the privelege of selling newspapers at Barking Station, but Messrs W. Smith and sons obtaining the monopoly of all Railway Stations, he could only sell outside the Station for some years, and he was supported by local townsfold[51]. He died in 1892 and the business is still carried on by his daughter.

Mr Moultrie, Grocer[52], now in 1908 resides at his branch shop in Tanner Street. (William Moultrie in 1913 obtained the £10 gift[53]). He was a seafaring man, but about 1872 he left the sea life and commenced to work up a private Tea round in Plaistow, East Ham & Barking. Mr Moultrie at this time lived at Plaistow. He

---

48 Thomas Forge, watch maker 10 East Street, stationer 27 Broadway. (Kelly's 1886). Forge also appears as Clerk to the Public Lighting and Watching Committee in the "Public Establishments" section.
49 Mary Forge, sail maker, Heath Street; John William, Thomas, Richard and Richard (junior)Forge, smack owners. (Pigot 1839).
50 Foresters' Friendly Society (Thomas Forge, Sec.), Town Hall, Broadway. (Kelly's 1886).
51 Townsfolk.
52 John Moultrie, grocer, 31 Broadway & at Tanner Street. (Kelly's 1886).
53 James Hayes, who died in 1821, left the sum of £4,000 in trust for the poor of the Parish of Barking. The gift – popularly known as Hayes's £10 gift – was distributed equally among six poor housekeepers and six other poor persons from Barking and Ilford (six in each town).*The book of Barking*. 1931. p.42.

MR FROGLEY'S BARKING: A FIRST SELECTION

had a struggle to get a living, but his connections increased and he eventually opened a small General shop in Denmark Terrace, East Ham, which was only a village then. From here he purchased the business in Barking, then carried on by a Mr Holden (and who removed and took a shop at Rainham, now carried on by his manager – Mr Maskell). Mr Moultrie lost his wife at this shop and he later married his late wifes sister – at that time illegal - but Mr Moultrie held strong religious views and was connected with the "Brethren". In consequence of this marriage he was not allowed fellowship with the "Brethren" but he organised a gathering in his own house. In business he has been very successful and for many years has resided in Tanner Street – purchasing an old residence there and building a shop at the side, and also has now the Post Office attached. Mrs Moultrie has recently died.

Pearsons, Butchers, see Churchyard.

The *George*. [Pages 349-352]

Although this sign is very common in England it is said to be more rare in Essex. As to its origin opinions differs, but it originated no doubt from our patron Saint. The old house, was one of the oldest remaining in the Town, and its appearance certainly indicated that it was erected about the time of Elizabeth[54]. It was the old Coaching house – the London Coach started from this house, and the Landlord – Mr William White[55] - was also the owner of the Coach. In those days, that is previous to 1854, the inhabitants "coached" to London, or either walked there which was very often the case. Mr White drove the Coach twice daily to the "Bull" at Aldgate. It left Barking at 9.15 AM and 4.15 PM; returning at 12.30 PM and 7.30 PM. (In 1882 Mr White was residing at Tunbridge Wells with his nephew...). Luggage was mostly taken by carriers. The single fare from Barking to Aldgate was Outside 1/6, Inside 2/- (also see Railway).

In 1856 Mr James Holmes[56] – son of William Holmes, Builder of Axe Street – took possession of it [the George]. Mr Holmes was a Liberal in politics, which at that time – in Essex – for a publican was unique. In Essex there was

---

54 The George is mentioned in the survey of Barking carried out for King James I in 1609. Cyril Hart: *Barking town in 1609.*

55 William White, coach proprietor, Broadway. (Pigot 1839). William White, junior, George and coach proprietor. (White 1848).

56 James Holmes, George Hotel, & auctioneer, surveyor & appraiser, Broadway. (Kelly's 1874).

MR FROGLEY'S BARKING: A FIRST SELECTION

10 members of Parliament – all Conservatives - but in 1879-80 all Liberals was successful – to the delight of Mr Holmes. A personality such as he possessed would naturally result in such a person being at the top and a leader of men. Such was Mr Holmes, therefore it would fill a book to briefly state his life from 1856 to 1881. He was an expert bricklayer, builder, Auctioneer, Architect, Publican and goodness knows what. He was a great supporter of the "Fair" and all his life after its abolition he gave away Ginger Bread to his customers on the Festival days. In 1865 his first wife died here, and he married again to a widow – Mrs Bryant. On January 18th, 1881 – Black Tuesday – he had an Auction Sale at Woodford, but the severe snow storm prevented him getting there, but he contracted a cold which terminated his energetic life in November 1881[57]. His widow was embarresed by debts after his death, but she looked above them and soon cleared them off. Her business increased to an enormous extent in consequence of the Byfrons and other Estates being built upon. She continually enlarged the bars, dispensing with the tap-rooms and private rooms on the ground floor. She died in 1892[58]. The Lease it appears had ran out, so at her death the Brewers took possession previous to her death, and compensating her, they put in another tenant – Mr Bishop[59] – who undertook to pull down the house and erect on its site a large and modern structure. After the old house was demolished, the Local Board availed themselves of obtaining a strip of the vacant land to widen this corner and in 1891 the Brewers reluctantly sold a strip of their frontage for £300, which compelled the Brewers to purchase the shop adjoining in North Street of Mr Dawson, but the Tenant, who had had some 11 years to run of his lease demanded an exhorbitant price for it and which was refused by the Brewers. Mr Bishop who also possesses both the Public-Houses opposite the Fenchurch St Railway Station, built a new house and opened it in 1893.

Edward *Deveson*[60] **[Page 353]**

– Corn and Coal Merchant, Broadway, was manager to (and also a later

---

57   *St Margaret's churchyard: register of graves.* 1930. p.27.
58   *St Margaret's churchyard: register of graves.* 1930. p.27 gives date of death as 2nd December 1893.
59   Walter Henry Bishop, George P.H., Broadway. (Kelly's 1900).
60   Edward Deveson, corn & coal merchant, Broadway & Fisher Street. (Kelly's 1886). Died 1890. *St Margaret's churchyard: register of graves.* 1930. p.113.

MR FROGLEY'S BARKING: A FIRST SELECTION

successor to) Mr G. A. Burrell[61]. (Mr George Augustus Burrell, Farmer, Coal Merchant, resided in a large house in Tanner Street, and under the old Authority was Surveyor of Barking. He died 11th August 1871 and is buried in Barking Churchyard). He [Edward Deveson] also had Manbridge Wharf, Fisher Street. He was in his manner severe, and I am informed that previous to his death, he decided to sell the business in the Broadway, and his son Charles[62] wished to take it and pay his father from the profits of the business. But he opposed his son having it and was decided upon the point. However Mr Edward Harriss[63] (already mentioned) purchased it, but the purchase was not for himself, but for the son Charles Deveson – unbeknown and to the surprise of his father. Edward Deveson died in August 1890 and Charles – his son – paid back Mr Harris and has recently retired from business.

The Barge Aground (See Market House).

Robert Willett [64] – son of Mr John Willett – and whom he succeeded. As a young man he was one of the most energetic men in local affairs. He succeeded to his fathers "Pawnbroking" business in the old Workhouse buildings, but has shut that up and carries it on at the old Infant School. Also the old National School he acquired for furniture. In the Broadway he purchased the Drapery business – next to the Congregational Church, also the Hosiers shop opposite. (This shop was a Pawnbrokers for many years, and kept by Mr William Budd who died in 1879).

Opposite the Bull – at the corner of Church Path - was a small lean-too shop used as a greengrocers by Mr Edward Sutton (not Samuel) and from here is a fine row of new shops. This site was a field occupied by Mr Howes, and who also had a saw pit on it. (This I believe was the last of the many saw pits that once graced Barking. Mr Howes, after leaving Barking went to the Kings Arms, at Grays Essex – After Mr Howes left the saw-pits, Mr C. Clark[65] ship breaker had the grounds). On this ground was a fine chesnut Tree, over-lapping North Street. In the rear was 3 old wooden houses painted

---

61 George Augustus Burrell, corn, coal & lime merchant, Fisher Street & Tanner Street. (Kelly's 1874). Surveyor & Churchwarden, 1854-67. *Barking vestry minutes*, p.318.
62 Charles Deveson, 28 Longbridge Road. (Kelly's 1895); corn merchant, 14 Broadway & 118 East Street. (Kelly's 1900).
63 Edward Harris, 201 North Street. (Kelly's 1895).
64 Robert Willett, linen draper, Broadway. (Kelly's 1886).
65 Charles Clark, lighterman, reed grower, shipbroker, dealer in English oak, ship & other timber & manure, Winning Horse, New Road & opposite the Bull, North Street. (Kelly's 1886).

BROADWAY - E side. (See page 36)
Page 348 in the manuscript.

Page 350 - 351 in the manuscript. (See page 38)

The Fishing Smack in about 1898. (See page 55)

Henry and Elizabeth Seabrook of the Fishing Smack (middle rear). (See page 55)

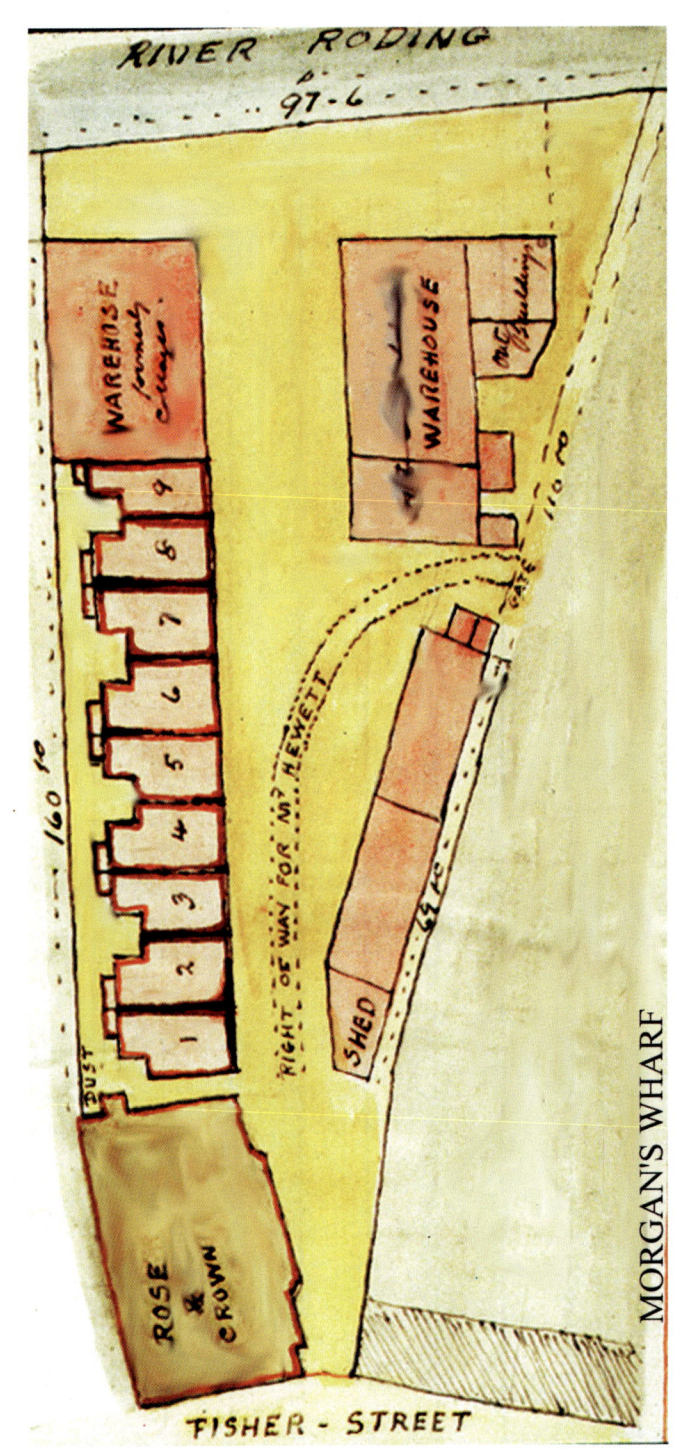

Page 383 in the manuscript. (See page 56)

MORGAN'S WHARF

The bascule bridge. Frogley inserted a similar photograph on page 384 of the manuscript. (See page 57) A description of the bridge appears in *Barking Record*, no. 74, 1967.

Plan of ABBEY JUTE MILL 1891

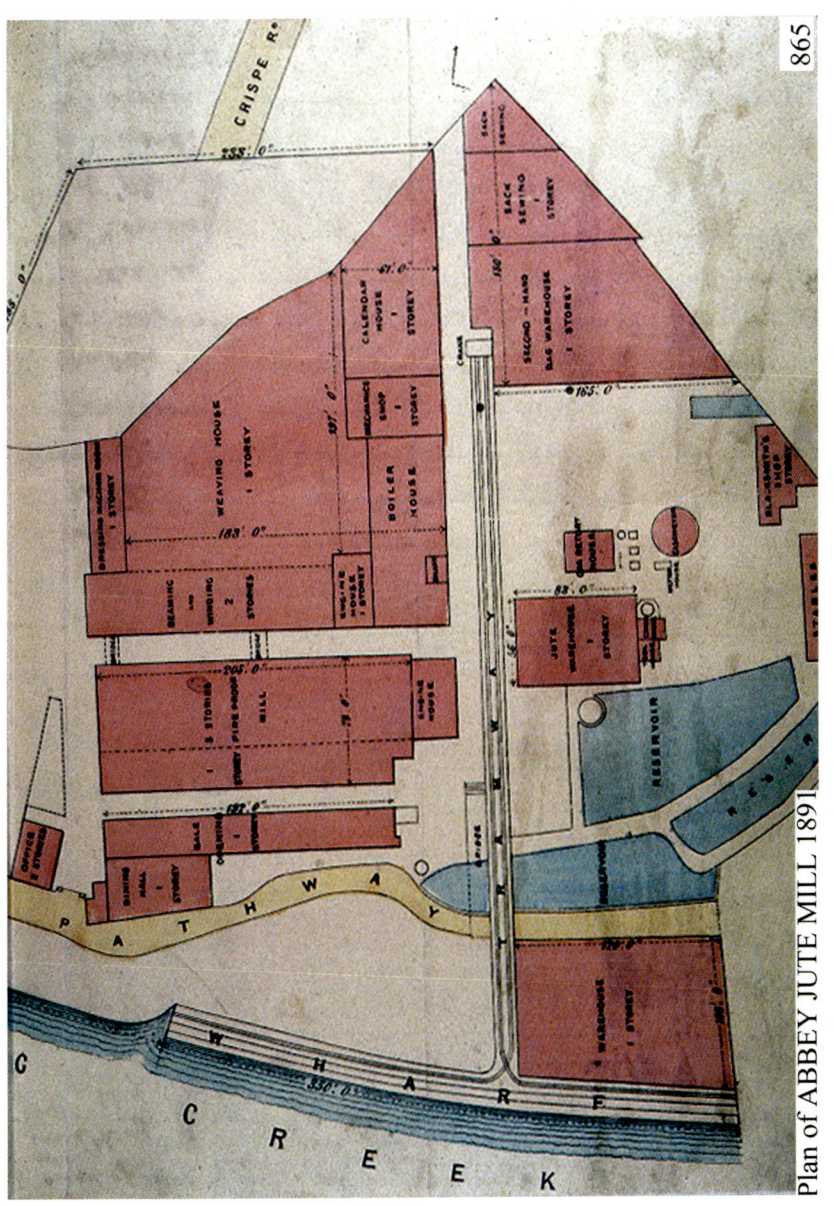

Page 387 in the manuscript, where Frogley gives the year as 1895, although the text refers to 1891. (See page 58).

RE-OPENING
OF
BARKING JUTE WORKS.

THESE

WORKS WILL BE OPENED

ON OR ABOUT

THE 19TH INSTANT.

WOMEN AND CHILDREN

Over 14 Years of Age

WISHING EMPLOYMENT

Can have their Names Registered at once by applying at the Works.

Barking, March 5th, 1888.

866

A clipping from the Essex Times, March 1888, on page 386 of the manuscript.
(See page 59)

MR FROGLEY'S BARKING: A FIRST SELECTION

white, let at 6/-, 4/6 and 4/- weekly, also a few brick cottages. These were demolished in 1894 and the new shops erected – abutting North Street.

The *Broadway* [Page 354]

– immediately opposite the George Inn it was kerbed and Metalled in 1885; and has always been the spot for the people to gather. During the "Fishery time" this was undoubtedly the most busy part. In the centre of the road was a lamp – or three lamps on one stem - here it was and is now customary to hold meetings of all classes. The lamp was removed and a public convenience erected at a cost of £2291, but as there was so many complaints it [the convenience] was removed in March 1896 and the lamp again erected at a cost of £65.

Austin Mays – Bookseller, Stationer etc. 57 Broadway[66]. He was formerly an Employee of the Jute Works, but similar to many others, when those works closed, took shops or opened up some business in the Town. (Also see Royal Oak). He took the Royal Oak in 1890 and Mr F. Clarke succeeded him in the shop.

Thomas Young. Auctioneer[67]. Another employee of the Jute Works. He was an engine fitter. After the closing of the jute works in [ ] he turned his attention to House repairs, and success following him he also collected rents & finally became an Auctioneer. His offices is now (1906) over the newsagents shop at the corner of Church Path. His name will often be met with in connection with the Local Bodies and other societies with which he has associated with.

Barking Distillery - Broadway – [Page 354]

was formerlly an old wooden-house entered by steps and its sign was the Queens Head – all these signs "Queens Heads" is mostly named after Elizabeth. About 1873 the old house was destroyed by fire. Another house was built, and for many years a family named "Gray" had it. Mr Gray[68] – a very heavy drinker – died in December 1887, and his widow died there in November 1889. The house was sold to Mr Charles Gibbons – who also had

---

66   Austin Mays, stationer, 57 Broadway. (Kelly's 1886, 1894).

67   Thomas Young, mechanical engineer, Linton Road. (Kelly's 1886); auctioneer, house & estate agent, 20 Broadway & 9 Linton road. (Kelly's 1894).

68   John Crowder Gray, Queen's Head P.H., Broadway. (Kelly's 1886).

MR FROGLEY'S BARKING: A FIRST SELECTION

the Prince Arthur, Rathbone Street, Canning Town – for £550 and the following year he made extensive alterations both internally and externally at a cost of £1500 and renamed the house "The Barking Distillery". In 1894 he made a good bargain when he sold it to a Mr Bundock[69], and who in 1896 sold it again to Mr Bates[70].

Back Lane. [Page 355]

This very narrow lane, or passage, runs paralell with North Street, but that portion from the Church Gates to Barking Road – although very old – yet I suggest is more modern than the other part, in fact, when the Town Hall was erected, undoubtedly there was no other building on this spot except the old house in Church Path, which faced the pond at one time. The houses backing on to the Churchyard is very old, and portions of some of them is much older than the Town-Hall. On Nos 13 and 15 is the date 1779, but the adjoining house – from the carving and general appearance of the internal portion - suggests them to have been the quarters, or kitchens for the old Monks.

The Mariners Arms[71] – Back Lane – at the rear of the Town Hall was a low ceilinged house and had a frontage of about 25 feet with one entrance, but the bar and Taproom was large. It was closed up in 1907. The residents of Back Lane are mostly street hawkers and bird fanciers[72].

Barking Fair. [Pages 369-370]

Before closing the account of North Street, the above annual Festival – now an institution of the past – should be mentioned. Originally, we are told that the origin of Fairs sprang entirely from the Church. They were really annual Markets and was held in the Churchyards. The days on which they were held was mostly the Festival day of some "Saint" when the people came and bought and sold; but as time went on, these Fairs with their attendant circumstances became intolerable as a religious institution, and the Church being unable to satisfactorilly regulate its business, the scene of the Fairs changed to the "Market Places".

---

69 Philip Bundock, Queen's Head P.H., Broadway. (Kelly's 1894).
70 Alfred Ernest Bates, Queen's Head P.H., 16 Broadway. (Kelly's 1900).
71 The 1881 census shows the Mariners Arms beerhouse in Back Lane kept by Joseph Freeman. Later Kelly's and other sources show this was 13 Back Lane.
72 For example, Henry Barnard, bird fancier, 7 Back Lane and John Porter, bird fancier, 14 Back Lane. (Kelly's 1900).

MR FROGLEY'S BARKING: A FIRST SELECTION

The days on which Barking Fair was held was October 22nd, 23rd & 24th, the Festival days of St Ethelburga, the first Abbess of Barking. The Fair was distributed all over the Town, but the chief centre - that contained the various "Shows", Stalls, Shooting galleries and travelling theatres - occupied the whole of the West side of North Street from the "George Inn" to the London Road, while the horses, donkeys &c was distributed all over the town, and the writer has seen yearly, hundreds of these animals at each Fair, and it was very amusing to see the fishermen and their wives having donkey rides. Most of the Public Houses, that had ground in their rear, had booths erected for dancing – in fact for three days the aspect of the town represented some gigantic carnival. On the horse-pond – adjoining the old Abbey wall - generally stood Wombells travelling Managerie[73]. Also Waxwork and other shows with the usual handsome decorated fronts. Opposite the George usually stood "Fredericks" travelling theatre. This man was grandfather of the "Fredericks" who own now the Borough Theatre and Theatre Royal Stratford[74].

Between these two spots was the various stalls – some of the owners of which was respectable tradesmen of East London. Ginger Bread and Ginger Nuts (Biscuits) was a speciality of the Fair. Also many old inhabitants possess useful articles – vases - &c – That was purchased from these stalls. But there came a time when some of the Religious bodies decided if possible to rid Barking of one of its most ancient festivals, and accordingly they managed to get a numerously signed petition which was sent to the Home Secretary who issued an Order for its abolition. The last fair was held in 1874, and in October 1875 the Police was stationed at the roads leading into the town and turned back the showmen, who evidently was not aware of this new Order.

Mr James Holmes of the George Inn was a great supporter of the fair, and in commemoration he gave away to his customers Ginger Bread and Nuts, and

---

[73] "Captain" George Wombwell (d.1850) started his travelling menagerie in 1807, when he was 30 years old. His first exhibit was two boa constrictors, bought on the London docks for £50. He wandered from one end of Britain to the other with his animals; eventually his show became so large that it had to be divided into three units. After his death, the show continued for many years in the hands of his nieces and nephews, some of whom were called Bostock.

[74] Albert Fredericks became general manager of the Theatre Royal, Stratford, in April 1888. The Fredericks family, the brothers Fred and Albert, and their children and in-laws, were one of the largest managerial families in the East End. The Theatre Royal passed out of the family's hands in 1957. Interestingly the space opposite the George became the site of the first cinema in Barking – the Bioscope may have dated back to 1912.

MR FROGLEY'S BARKING: A FIRST SELECTION

after his death in 1881, his widow[75] continued the custom until her death in [ ]. All fairs were markets, although all markets are not fairs, and the profits from the rent of Stalls &c I understand belonged to the "Market House" or Fanshawes charity, but singularly it was chiefly by the Trustees of that Charity signing the Petition, that the Fair was abolished.

Fisher Street. [Pages 377-392]

This now very uninviting thoroughfare was during the time of the Fishery trade the most important street in the town. The following letter from an old inhabitant will bear out the above statement. Mr Auckland, of Bishopsgate Street, E.C.[76] – formerly of Barking - wrote in 1898: "I recall the Barking days of my youth as the happiest of life. How fragrant was Heath & Fisher Streets, with the smell of the Pitch & Tar – how well the Stores was stocked with oil-skins: top-boots: Guernseys: Rope & Red-caps &c &c. These times have changed – old associations disappeared, everything becoming new – but even the old state of things in Barking is preferable".

Anyone who knew Fisher Street in that day will agree with every word of Mr Auckland. Running parallel with the river, it will always command that trade usually connected with Wharves.

---

75 Mrs Mary Ann Holmes, George Hotel, Broadway. (Kelly's 1886).
76 Thomas F. Auckland, of 80 Bishopsgate Within. He contributed an article "Reminiscences of a fishing town" in *Essex Review*, 1900, Vol.9, p.185-6 : "Although born within the sound of Bow Bells, and thus supposed to be cockney by birth, I was never so much in my element as when at Barking among the fishermen and smacks. Those pretty vessels, the Ranger, Racer, Leander, Ocean Pacific, Blue Bell, Tartar, Saucy Lass, Transit, and a veritable host of others are as fresh in my memory as when they were afloat, and I recall the Barking days of my youth as among the happiest of my life. How fragrant Heath Street and Fisher Street smelt of tar and pitch, how well the stores were supplied with sou'westers, oilskins, big-boots, guernseys, red caps, hawsers, ropes and twine. How the boys marched about the town at fair-time, and enjoyed the fun, as if there never were gales or high seas off the Doggerbank and the coast of Iceland. I sometimes wonder whether the fish is so well-handled with the steam-trawler, as it used to be with the old fashioned sailing trawler with her sails neatly trailed up, how she glided along gathering up the fish so deftly and well! In those days Mr Samuel Hewitt used to drive to town in the eventide, starting from Barking about 6p.m., in an old-fashioned gig drawn by a white horse. He had a residence on Tower Hill, and this was a convenience for him, as he was needed in Billingsgate very early in the morning to meet the consignments of fish from the North Sea. I learn that recently the Short Blue fleet has been sold, and this fishing squadron so long associated with Barking creek has passed into the hands of the Dutch, our neighbours who have challenged us in former days in our own waters. Will they make the old sailing vessels pay, when our men have relinquished them in favour of steam? I just remember the Hon. and Rev. Robert Liddell being the Vicar of

MR FROGLEY'S BARKING: A FIRST SELECTION

Barking Cross Tavern. [Page 377]

The space facing this house was called the "Cross-Trees" – from a mast with cross-trees that originally stood in the centre of the road. At that time the sign of this house was the "Still" (an appropriate sign for a Spirit Merchants) & it occurs in the "Distillers Arms": As the Still it flourished during the Fishery time – but when that trade left the Town it was doomed. The old house "The Still" was entered by ascending 3 steps (nearly all the licenced houses had steps at that time in Barking) & was occupied by Mr John Ringer[77] who died there & was succeeded by his widow. (Mr Ringer died 1848. Mrs Rebecca Ringer his widow leaving the Still resided in Tanner Street but some years previous to her death built the house in Station Road – corner of James Street - & where she died in 1877. Both are buried in the Churchyard). She [Mrs Ringer] disposed of it [the Still] to Luke Horsley[78] – who had it in 1850 – but he was unsuccessful & lost his money. His sister in law – Mrs Ringer – allowed him £1 a week till his death.

The next owner was Mr Henry Earle[79], who married Miss Frogley[80] – Aunt of the writer. Mr Earle was a Mast & block maker, boat builder &c and his father a Smack-owner. Henry Earle erected in the rear of the house a "look out" by which he could watch the incoming & outgoing vessels from & into the Thames. He was successful here. In 1858 Burglars entered & took away value of £131. Disposing of the Still he retired to private – but carried on his trade. He sold the house in 1865. Living in Church Road his only daughter died - & after which he removed to Grimsby where he had some vessels & where he died in [ ]. His widow – well provided for – removed to Camden Town, London, where she died in 1883 & was buried in the Congregational Burial Ground. The trade of the house got worse & worse & ultimately in

---

> Barking, and my uncle, the Rev. J. W. Charlesworth, preaching in St Margaret's Church. There was the old-fashioned square pew where the family all sat round with nothing in front of them. I have often travelled from the Bull Inn, Aldgate, on top of the coach, with Mr W. White (who we call Billy White), and he tooled a four-horse team very well".

77 John Ringer, Still, Fisher Street. (Pigot 1839, White 1848).

78 Luke Horsley, smack owner & mast, oar, block & pump maker, Fisher Street. (Pigot 1839).

79 Henry Earl, smack owner, Fisher Street. (Pigot 1839, White 1848); Henry William Earle, Still. (White 1863). East of London Family History Society:*1851 census index series*: vol.1, pt.4: Barking. 1984. p.12.

80 Mary Anne Frogley (1822-1883).

MR FROGLEY'S BARKING: A FIRST SELECTION

1882 it was closed up. ... The Brewers re-opened it under management for a short time, when a tenant was obtained named Charles Carey. Rent £40. He however failed. During the year (1882) the floors was lowered to the road level & the house re-named the Cross-Trees Tavern & later Barking Cross Tavern. Mr Carey sold the house to a Mr Earnie for £50 in 1883 who in April 1885 sold it to Mr Silvester – recently come from Africa. He however brought proceedings against Earnie for mis-representation & eventually the house closed again later in 1885. How long it was closed I do not know, but it was open in 1887 & the tenant a Mr Peter Reynolds[81] – who came from a Beer-house at the corner of Red-post Lane & Romford Road (now closed up). He sold it in 1898 to Miss Bates. In 1912 (June) it was finally closed & in October 1912 opened as a Mission Hall by the Baptists.

Rose & Crown – for many years tenanted by a family named Milton. In 1850 Mrs Milton[82] – widow – kept it & her son Frederick[83] was the principal Bass singer at the Church. About 1878 there was a big flood at this pub (see Floods) & Fred Milton waddling in the water contracted a cold that caused his death. A later tenant Mr C. Walesby[84] from the Chequers, Dagenham Road, sold it in 1890 to Mr Benson & who again sold it in 1896 to Mr Duck. He sold it in 1897 to Mr Barden[85]. In 1899 a Mr Creed was Tenant & he sold it in 1900 to a Mr Oliver. The house was closed up in March 1904 & since demolished.

The *Fishing Smack* [Page 378]

– a sign in evidence of a fishing town was many years past tenanted by a family named Bauckham[86]. This family by trade was Shipwrights – boat-builders - but the descendants now (1900) are mostly in the Decorating trade & very poor. Bauckham was succeeded by Mr Henry Seabrook[87] in 1863.

---

81 *Essex almanac for 1889* gives name as John Reynolds, as does Kelly's 1890. Mrs Jane Reynolds is listed in 1900.
82 Louisa Milton, died at Gorleston in 1880. *St Margaret's churchyard: register of graves.* 1930. p.85.
83 Died 1874. *St Margaret's churchyard: register of graves.* 1930. p.85.
84 Charles Edmund Walesby, Rose & Crown P.H., Fisher Street. (Kelly's 1890). Died 1896. *St Margaret's churchyard: register of graves.* 1930. p.222.
85 Charles A. Barden, Rose & Crown, 36 Fisher Street. (Kelly's 1900).
86 Various entries in *St Margaret's churchyard: register of graves.* 1930. Edwin Bauckham, tailor, 5 Fisher Street. (Kelly's 1886).
87 Henry Seabrook, Fishing Smack P.H., Fisher Street. (Kelly's 1886, 1890). His eldest son, Henry Thomas Seabrook, Chief Engineer of the SS Hornby Grange, died on board of apoplexy at sea near the equator in 1895, and was buried at sea. *St Margaret's churchyard: register of graves.* 1930. p.226.

MR FROGLEY'S BARKING: A FIRST SELECTION

Being a Smith – he also has a "Smiths Shop" at the rear of the house. The house was then also entered by ascending steps, but Mr Seabrook had the floors lowered. He was successful here & was enabled to own some Freehold houses in East Street which he built. Dying in November 1899 his Widow & daughter continued the Business[88]. In 1901 the house was pulled down & rebuilt & Mrs Seabrook retired from the Business on account of her age in 1906[89]. Their tenancy was 43 years.

The Malt-House – built in 1866 for Messsrs Randall & Co[90] – but since then has been enlarged by taking over a portion of Donkey Park.

Donkey Park – a field adjoining the Malt-House & for many years apparently having no legal owner – similar to other land in Barking. A portion of it is occupied by Mr Donaldson[91]– late Manager of the Jute Works - for engineering purposes.

The *Hope* [Page 383]

– near the Fishing Smack on the opposite side of the road, a small Beerhouse for many years owned by Mr Alfred Clark[92] – who previously had a wine stores – No 5 Heath Street – but after obtaining a Licence for the "Hope" in 1876 he gave up the wine stores & transferred his business to the Hope. In 1898 it was for sale - & offered as a surrender for a proposed larger house then building or to be built at the corner of Boundary & Gascoigne Roads near by.

Labys Alley – a small Alley or Court named after a Mr Laby[93] who resided at the corner of it & owned the 12 small cottages it contained. They were sold by Auction in 1880. A Marsh on which the Barking Outfall Works is built was called Labys Marsh.

The Volunteer – near the Gas-Works – a modern beer-house opened I believe by

---

88 The Fishing Smack was separated from Hewett's engine house across the yard by a fitters shop which took the full blast of a terrible explosion on 6th January 1899 which killed ten people. Henry Seabrook, who was in the pub taking a nap at the time, was so severely shocked by the explosion that it was said to have contributed to his death a few months later.
89 Elizabeth Charlotte Seabrook died in 1910. She and husband Henry reared eleven children including James Seabrook OBE, Lieutenant Commander RN, Acting Consul of Trieste in 1917 and Thomas Seabrook, who was "skipper" of the paddle boat in Barking Park.
90 Randells, Howell & Co., malt roasters, Fisher Street. (Kelly's 1874, 1890, 1900).
91 James Donaldson, engineer, Fisher Street. (Kelly's 1900).
92 Alfred Clark, beer retailer & lighterman, 147 Fisher Street. (Kelly's 1890, 1900).
93 James Laby, coal merchant, Fisher Street. (Pigot 1839).

MR FROGLEY'S BARKING: A FIRST SELECTION

Richard Aldous [94]. He was formerly a railway porter & opened a butchers shop in North Street & during the cold winter evenings sold hot meat pies from a basket. Later he took the Volunteer. While here some building was in course of construction with the Malt House opposite & it was his custom to take over the mens beer. One day in doing so he fell from the scaffolding & his injuries caused his death. At this time the house was a small cottage with a projecting Bar. In January 1889 the next shop – a bakers – caught fire & both houses were destroyed – except the projecting Bar – but this was pulled down. The Local Board decided that the new house should be built further back to meet the contemplated widening of this & other streets in the town. The Freeholder of this property however having died & his Will stated that the property could not be disposed of until his legatees was 25 years old & that would occur in 1894. It was finally decided that the Local Board should purchase 10 feet of the frontage in depth for £100 & the money put in trust until 1894. The House having been rebuilt the widow married again to a young man named Nicholls[95] & who became Landlord in 1889. Mrs Nicholls died about 1910.

Morgans Wharf – situated on the Roding. The greater part was purchased of Griffiths Taylor[96] in 1858 by Mr James Morgan[97] & the other part from a Mr Frederick White in 1863. In August 1892 this Wharf was offered for sale by Auction. It had a frontage of 95 feet to the River & comprised 2 Warehouses & 11 cottages. For several years two brothers named Sutton tenanted it as a coal wharf. The eldest Brother died in 1879 & Samuel[98] the youngest in 1893 failed or was unable to continue it. He still (1912) resides in Barking. (Mr Sutton Senior, father of the above, was during the fishery trade very successful as a mast & block maker & assisted his sons in the Coal Business when his own business left the town. He unfortunately died in great poverty in 1891 age 71). Messrs Boniface & Co Coal-Merchants took it & who with a Mr Barclay of Creekmouth commenced to trade there in 1893. In 1894 they were Bankrupt for £700. An account of the Morgan family is noticed under Fishery.

---

94 Family grave of Richard (d.1886) and Elizabeth Aldous in *St Margaret's churchyard: register of graves.* 1930. Richard Aldous, tripe dresser. (White 1863); beer retailer & baker, Fisher Street. (Kelly's 1886).

95 William Nichols, beer retailer, 113 Fisher Street. (Kelly's 1890).

96 Griffiths Taylor, shipwright, Barking. (Pigot 1839).

97 James Morgan, smack owner, Heath Street. (Pigot 1839).

98 Samuel Thomas Sutton, coal merchant, Fisher Street. (Kelly's 1890).

MR FROGLEY'S BARKING: A FIRST SELECTION

The *Battery Wharf* [99]. [Page 384]

This wharf took its name from he fact that in 1860 a new force called the "Naval Reserve" came into existence[100], for the better protection of the Country & all were eligible that had an experience of 5 years of sea life. Several Barking Fishermen joined. The inducement was £8 a year payable quarterly & if totaly disabled from following their employment or on reaching the age of 60 - they were to receive £12 a year. The above Wharf was then a bare field or meadow & on it was built a large wooden shed of two stories & the spot was called the Battery ground, where the Fishermen drilled. A "Gunboat" was also stationed in the Creek & on which about 30 Fishermen drilled daily. This only appeared to have lasted a few years in consequence of the Fishery trade leaving the Town. In 1898 a Company was formed, of which Mr Robert Hewett is Managing Director, who acquired this Wharf upon a Lease, expiring in 1925 from Mr Hewett, who had a private interest in it. The Company is called the River Roding Company. The Company also possessed other land here and at East Ham – the site of the East-Ham Outfall Works is their property. In January 1905 the Company brought an Action against the Barking Town Council claiming £10,000 as damage done to their Wharf trade in consequence of the new bridge having been erected against their land & which they say caused the larger vessels to cease coming to their Wharf.

The Mission Church – built in 1878 and estimated to seat 200 people. Several clubs & classes are connected with it. The officiating minister at that time was the Rev Vincent Smith[101].

The Hop-Pole – a beerhouse kept by a Mr John Howe, formerly owner of the saw-pits opposite the Bull Inn. It has been closed & demolished for some years. (While at the Hop-Pole, Mrs Howe had a mania for saving all the "Crown pieces" that came into her hand, unbeknown to her husband. She had a floor board taken up for the purpose of hiding the crown-pieces & by replacing the board no one was aware of what was accumalating there. But the Hop-Pole was disposed of & she then gathered up her hoard & to the surprise of herself &

---

99 Battery Wharf had been used originally for loading and storing the marsh ice for Hewett's Short Blue Fleet. After the main fishing fleet had left Barking for the east coast in the 1860s, the ice-houses were converted into engineering shops for servicing the steam fleet carriers.
100 Naval Reserve Gun Battery, Fisher Street. (Kelly's 1874).
101 Rev. Vincent Smith, A.K.C.I., Park House, Hart Street. (Kelly's 1886); 28 Fisher Street.

husband if was said that they decided with the money to build a cottage in the Wakering Road, Barking. This they did & it was named "Crown Cottage" as the name on a stone signified. This cottage was purchased & pulled down for the Railway Improvements in 1907. It was built in 1874).

Abbey Works (Jute factory). **[Pages 385-388]**

The Abbey Works – once popularly known as the Jute Works - is a noble pile of buildings at the extreme end of Fisher Street. In the year 1866 – about the time when the staple industry – the Fishery – was leaving the town – the inhabitants rejoiced to hear of how a large jute manufacturing firm was to be stationed in the town. These works was erected by Mr Thomas Duff of Scotland for jute manufacturing purposes. The acreage of the land occupied by & attached to these buildings is about [12.75] acres & the combined buildings was said to be one of the largest jute works in the Kingdom – the water frontage to the Roding is 910 feet. The buildings consists of a spacious fire-proof Mill of 3 stories high, 78 feet wide & 205 feet long & contains two lifts. Another building 183 feet wide & 197 feet long has a partly glassed roof supported by strong iron columns. Other buildings include the Boiler shop, Mechanics shop, Dining room & other extensive buildings including the Offices & the Shalf[102] – 170 feet high – make the whole a very imposing block.

The site of these works was marshland owned by a Mrs Nash, but of course after the works was built, houses also multiplied. Singularly an Englishman - Mr Mills – was the first manager, but after a few years he left Barking to take up the management of similar works at Ponders End. His successor was a rank Scotchman – Mr Alexander[103] - & for years the works progressed satisfactorily. In 1876 spacious Dining rooms was erected for the employees & a library added to it by Messrs Levy & Co, who purchased the works from Mr Duff in 1875. Prosperity continued until 1886 when foreign competition & other causes resulted in the business falling off in an appalling manner. During 1887 unfortunately the Company was compelled to close the works as it was then worked at a loss and the machinery was in a bad state of repair.

(Kelly's 1890). Frogley covers Smith's career under "Curates" on page 117 of the manuscript. For Smith's work with the Fisher Street Mission, including the minute book (1877-1887), see Essex Record Office D/P 81/28/30-37.

102 Frogley probably intended to write "Shaft".
103 John Alexander, manager, Jute Manufactory. (Kelly's 1874).

MR FROGLEY'S BARKING: A FIRST SELECTION

At this time & for years past over 1200 persons were daily employed there – in addition to hundreds who fetched the cloth to their homes to sew into bags (or sacks). Thus sometimes whole families was engaged.

In March 1888 the works was re-opened & at a Meeting held in London this month of the Company, the Company was grieved to know that Mr Barclay – Managing Director for 21 years – was about to resign – as by losing him it was felt the whole concern was doomed. In the following April 1889 – Levy & Co – with their limited capital - found it impossible to continue on with the Works & decided to sell the whole concern to a Mr John H. Ward for £32,500. It was rumoured that Mr Ward was really a nominee for Mr Barclay. Wether true or not, Mr Barclay unfortunately died on the day the purchase was completed – after an operation at his residence at Hackney. Also this year (1889) Mr Alexander – the Manager – resigned & Mr Donaldson (Under-Manager) succeeded him. Although their was trouble in making the Works there was several strikes during 1888-9 which resulted in a general lock-out in 1889. Eventually the employees was glad to return upon any terms. The last Annual Excursion took place in 1889 when – headed by the town-band – the employees marched to the Railway Station & went by special train to Tilbury. It had previously been the Custom to head the procession with some Scotch-Pipers.

In March 1891 the works was again offered for sale & a notice posted on the gates that they would be closed on March 26th. About 1400 was then employed there, & so keen was it felt by the Workpeople (& Tradesmen) that the former forwarded a petition stating they were willing to work for 10% less wages, but as the new Company had already lost £20,000 the Directors replied that they could not any further carry on the works & which was finally closed in April. The various religious bodies – especially the Congregationialists – opened relief stations & by their aid most of the foreign employees were assisted to their homes. These foreign Employees is explained in the foot-note. (At the opening of the works in 1866-7 several Scotch lasses, versed in jute manufacture was imported from Dundee – but the greatest number that came down from Scotland & Ireland was in consequence of the various strikes that occurred for many years previous to those of 1888-9. Some had previously gone back & got married, but there were a great many stranded in Barking when the Works finally closed up. Some was assisted to Canada). In June 1891 the works was again offered for sale, but there was no bidding, & in July 1891 a four days sale by Auction was held at which the Machinery-Plant &c was sold.

MR FROGLEY'S BARKING: A FIRST SELECTION

At the time of the Auction Sale the works contained amongst other articles: 25 Breaking-Machines: 20 Roving Machines: 30 Spinning-frames: 27 Drawing-Machines: 35 Sewing & Hemming ditto: 216 Looms: 7 Calender Machines: besides double Spinning frames & some 100 other Machines of various types.

Mr Howe of Barking[104] – rope & twine maker – but for many years an employee of & also Forman at the Jute works, but similar to others, when the works closed, commenced business on his own account. Also Mr Thomas Young Auctioneer &c and Austin Mays[105], tobacconist, but now a publican - was employees at the Jute works till it closed. Mr Howe however has wrote a small book or pamphlet[106] on Jute Manufacture – which described the process that it underwent at these works until the cloth or canvas was made & ready for sacks &c &c. He says:- Jute chiefly grown in India (British) is made into bales & conveyed to this country. After which it is opened by Machinery & passed through a Softener – then through the Breakers called Carding – then through another Card or Combing Machine called Finisher. It runs from this into Cans, and from these Cans to the Drawing & Roving Machines which seperate it & is now called Rove – passing on to the Bobbing. The next process is the Spinning & finally the Weaving Machines.

In July 1891 the above equipment was all sold – leaving the Factory entirely empty & as such for offered for sale at the "Mart" with a reserve of £20,000. The writer attended this sale. There was no bidding so it was bought in at that figure. It was shortly afterwards (January 1896) purchased by Messrs Warne & Co of Tottenham[107] – the well known Rubber Manufacturers & since then I am informed they have removed their business entirely from Tottenham to Barking. About 1000 hands are employed – principally all adults - & in 1908 they were the largest customer for Electric-Lighting the Council had.

Sale of wharves. [Page 389]

In 1895 several wharves & land abutting on the River Roding was offered for sale by Auction among which was the sites of the following factories, Wharves &c :-

---

104 William Howe, sack & bag manufacturer, Town Quay. (Kelly's 1900).
105 Austin Mays, stationer, 57 Broadway & 117 East Street. (Kelly's 1900).
106 Howe, William *A paper on jute and its manufacture*. Wilson & Whitworth, 1891.
107 William Warne & Co. Ltd, India rubber goods manufacturers, India Rubber Mills, Fisher Street. (Kelly's 1900).

MR FROGLEY'S BARKING: A FIRST SELECTION

1. Site of the Patent Cork Company – for paving purposes. These works was destroyed by fire in August 1894. Damage estimated at £3000. The River frontage to this site is 335 feet.
2. The Economising & Improved Light Syndicate.
3. Hewetts Wharf – Plan on next page – River frontage 230 feet. The site was formerly the Freehold of Messrs Ind Coope & Co of Romford, Brewers. They still retain the site of the Fishing Smack.
4. Bleak House – a large brick house very old & containing ten rooms – with 8 acres of land.
5. A Wharf containing [1.5] acres & a River frontage of 222 feet.
6. A Wharf containing 3 acres & a River frontage of 370 feet.
7. A Wharf containing 5 acres & a River frontage of 340 feet.
8. A Wharf containing 6 acres and a River frontage of 350 feet.

Also Morgans Wharf already noticed. All these Wharves were during the middle of the 19th century apparently thriving – depending successively upon the needs of the Town through the Fishery Trade – But the various factories & works that have since that time occupied them have mostly been failures.

Hewetts Explosion [108]. [Pages 389-392]

In closing the account of Fisher Street there is a very melancholy event to record. On 6th January 1899 a terrible explosion occurred at Messrs Hewetts yard & which resulted in the closing of the yard. The explosion which was felt for miles round was occassioned by the Bursting of an old boiler, that originally did duty on one of the Firms Steam Trawlers till 1890. In 1892 it was put into repair & fixed at their works in Fisher Street. It apparently worked well until 1896, but in 1897 it was again repaired, but extraordinarily not used again until the day of the accident. Such was the force of the explosion that thick walls was shattered to peices - strong iron twisted – roofs stripped &c &c. The view on page [ ] shows a large piece of iron – a plate – hurled nearly a quarter of a mile – crashing through a wall of a house occupied by a Mr Decker, going through the bed room floor into the kitchen

---

108 According to Archie Seabrook, grandson of Henry, one victim of the explosion was Jim Harden, who gained for himself the title of "The man they could not kill". He was blown through the dividing wall into the skittle alley of the Fishing Smack, where he came to rest among heaps of wreckage and was missing for several hours. After the rubble had been cleared away, Jim was discovered with various injuries, but was quite disappointed that the blast had not carried him a few yards further into the tap room!

MR FROGLEY'S BARKING: A FIRST SELECTION

& finally into 2 feet of earth. The family had just got up from their dinner when it occurred. But by far the most lamentable part was the terrible loss of life, 10 being killed & several injured. A list of these unfortunate people is:-

1. Burness, Archibald – foreman engineer – of Barking.
2. Marshall, William. Blacksmith of Barking.
3. Pratten, G. J. Blacksmith of Barking.
4. Lloyd, Edward. Engineer of Smithfield (East).
5. Grant, Alfred. Apprentice of East-Ham.
6. Thornton, James & Sullivan, John. Both died in Popal[109] Hospital.
7. Hume, Arthur. Apprentice. Son of Local Organist, Barking[110].
8. Page, William of Barking. His body was found 4 days after the Accident in the Fitters shop underneath some rubbish – having been blown through a Wall.
9. Taylor, William. Blacksmith, from Poplar. Buried in East London Cemetery.

A Committee was formed to raise funds on behalf of the Bereaved & £2085.6.8 was collected within the year, and after deducting temporary allowances & other sums a sum amounting to £1599.17.6 as left for allocation. £200 was granted to each Widow & various other sums to the injured. The temporary allowances amounted to £444.15.10 and out of which it was neccessary to deduct £90.13.4 for outstanding liabilities, thus leaving the amount stated. Where there was families the money was invested by the Trustees.

Heath-Street. [Pages 393-396]

This short street is in continuation of North Street & leads to the "Quay". In appearance it now has a very dilapidated & forsaken condition, but during the reign of the Fishery Trade it had a very prosperous appearance. Although the shops was small there was few – if any – tradesmen residing there at that time but what amassed money. There was Ship-chandlers – boat builders – oilskins – and other dealers there doing a good business & there must have been more traffic in this short street than any other in the town. Old inhabitants have informed me of the seats in front of the houses, & how the Fishermen & others enjoyed their pipes outside.

The street is probably named after the Heath family[111]. Sir Thomas Fanshawe

---

109 Poplar?
110 Arthur Hume, organist of St Margaret's Church, 7 Cambridge Road. (Kelly's 1894, 1900).
111 Heath Street is actually named from "the hithe", a landing place on the river-bank, since it leads to the Town Quay. *Place names of Essex.* 1935. p.89.

MR FROGLEY'S BARKING: A FIRST SELECTION

married Margaret, daughter of Sir Edward Heath, whose father Robert Heath of Cotteamors[112] of Rutlands in 1649 was laying ill at Calais and was visited by his son without permission & was obliged to obtain consent to return home & Mr Gascoyne was surety for the Captain, who was his friend.

Hockleys shop – Mr Daniel Hockley occupied two shops at the corner of Hart Street which was built in 1842. Mr Hockley commenced business as a Draper & Clothier in 1858 & was very successful. Many years later he opened a Pawnbrokers in North Street, but he just previously went to reside at Chigwell, Essex & in June 1886 removed to West-Malling, Kent, where 2 months later he died age 53 and was buried at Tonbridge Cemetery. These two shops in Heath Street has been closed for years[113].

Weatheralls Court. At the corner of this Court was a small shop & Mr James Weatherall[114] – a short, stout man - was the proprietor & also owner of the few houses in the Court. He sold, & amassed money in the sale of, oilskins &c - the usual Fishermans outfit. He died in July 1879 and was buried in the Churchyard. He left £100 to the poor. His old housekeeper "Rebecca Belshams" an eccentric old lady after became an inmate of the Almshouses & at her death was buried in the same grave.

Stanley House. This large square plain bricked house stood behind the Ship Inn & was scarcely visible from Heath Street. It was approached through one of their narrow Courts. I know little of the Stanleys, as Mr Stanley died in 1810 & his sons later went to Australia & did not return until about 18[—?] to claim the property. Most of the small property adjoining the House belonged to this family. The Lake family was related to the Stanleys & they appeared to have managed the property while the sons was abroad. They found the large house nearly demolished, as for some 50 years the house was empty & anyone who wanted timber or bricks went & took it until the house dissappeared altogether. The writer has seen wood &c taken away for firewood &c.

---

112 Should be Cottesmore. See: Howson, James *Fanshawe family and other portraits*. 1983.
113 Mrs Emmeline Mary Hockley, pawnbroker, Broadway; & linen draper & clothier, 13, 15 & 17 Heath Street. (Kelly's 1890, 1894).
114 *St Margaret's churchyard: register of graves*. 1930. p.5.

MR FROGLEY'S BARKING: A FIRST SELECTION

The Blue Anchor [115] [Page 394]

– a sign of the Fishery Trade, it is a fully licenced house & the Anchor painted blue projected from the front. In 1814 the Landlord was Mr Joseph Frogley[116] – an ancestor of the writer – he was also a Smackowner. The house had a good garden in the rear. In 1876 the landlord was a James Grant[117], & he sold it to his Barman – Alfred Lovett – in 1877. In Feb 1897 a Mr Hardwick[118] (also a Councillor who had been in possession a long time and who was summoned for dilluting his Beer & he was convicted of negligence & carelessness). Mr Hardwick was in the house for many years & was highly respected & he was generally believed in his plea that he was victimised. It caused him to sell the business in 1897 to the present tenant – Mr H. Barnard[119].

The Commercial – a modern licence for Beer, was in 1882 tennanted by Mrs Elizabeth Binks, widow. Her husband died in 1876 at the "Victoria", Axe Street & in 1882 sold that house to take the "Commercial" – opposite was an old established Corn Business kept by Mr Gregory, a Congregationalist[120]. After his death Mr Wray purchased it … but closed it up in 1906 … having opened another business in Tanner Street. Mr Gregory was there for many years and is known for his religious principles.

Also opposite the "Commercial" resided Mr Robert Saggers[121] who commenced business here as an Undertaker in 1825. At the rear he had a

---

115 One of the oldest inns in the town. The will of Stephen Commynges (1588) refers to "my house near to the waterside in the town of Barking adjoining to the house called by the sign of the Blue Anchor". *Elizabethan life: home, work and land.* 1976. p.63. Also: "Johanna Fanshawe, widow, holds in free socage for the term of her life … a messuage by the common Wharfe of Barking, called the Blew Ancker". Cyril Hart, *Barking town in 1609.*

116 Joseph Frogley (1765-1847), a fisherman who married Elizabeth Mountgall (c.1767-1823) in 1788. His father, another Joseph (b.1740) married Jane Wells (b.1739) in 1764. Jane Wells was a legatee of Roger Vaughn (d.1756), brandy merchant, who had owned the Blue Anchor. Joseph and Elizabeth had two children – (1) Joseph (1789-1864), a fisherman, who married Ann Doous (d.1836) in 1815, and (2) Mary Ann (b.1799), who married Joseph Barnett in 1820, and died aged 20. *St Margaret's churchyard: register of graves.* 1930. p.163 records that near Mary Ann's grave "lieth the body of William Frogley, son of Mr John & Ann Frogley, who died October 7th, 1834, aged 4 years".

117 William Smith, Blue Anchor. (Pigot 1839). James Grant, Blue Anchor, Heath Street. (Kelly's 1874). Thomas Monk is listed in 1848 and Thomas Porter in 1863 (White).

118 Joseph Frederick Hardwick, Blue Anchor P.H., Heath Street. (Kelly's 1890, 1894).

119 Robert Barnard, Blue Anchor P.H., 52 Heath Street. (Kelly's 1900).

120 John Gregory, corn dealer, 2 Heath Street. (Kelly's 1874, 1890).

121 Robert Saggers, builder, carpenter & undertaker, Heath Street. (Pigot 1839). *St Margaret's churchyard: register of graves.* 1930. p.228.

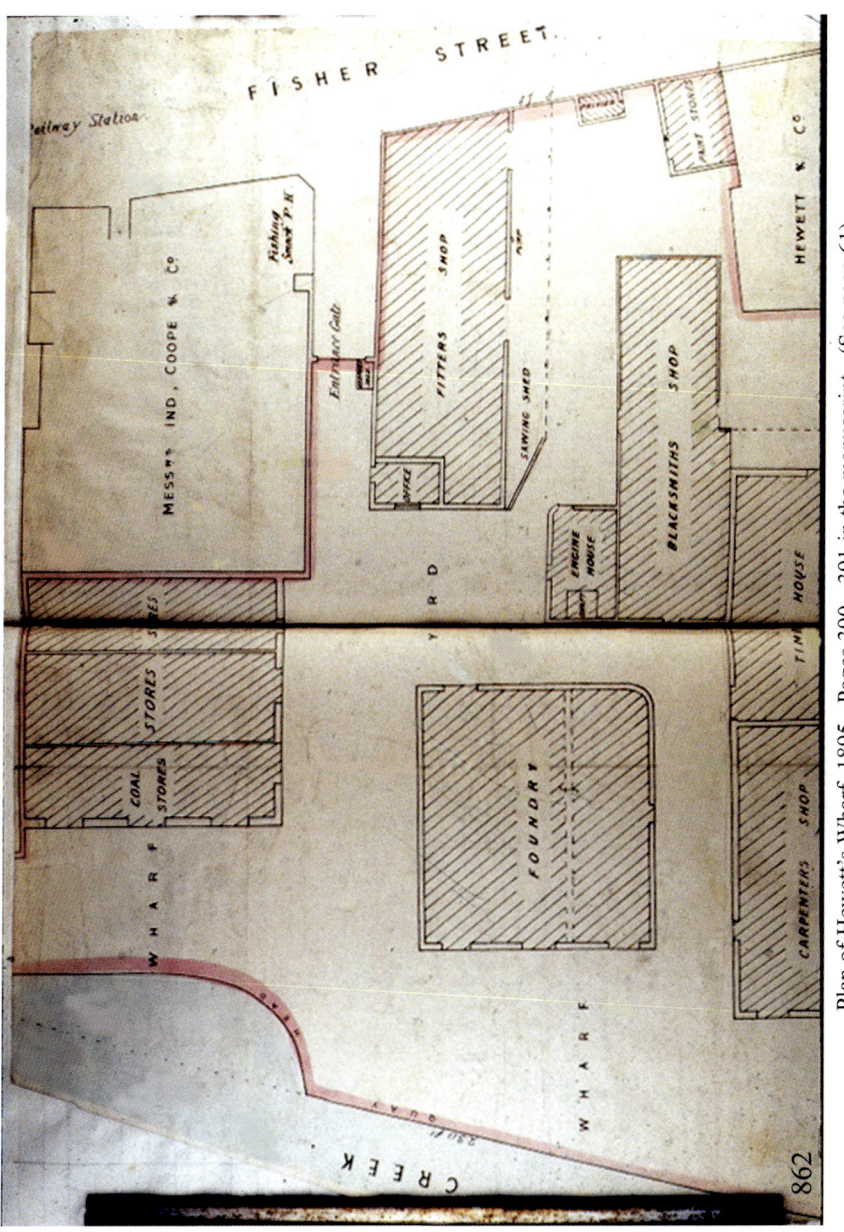

Plan of Hewett's Wharf, 1895. Pages 390 - 391 in the manuscript. (See page 61)

The explosion at Hewett's factory. Page 392 in the manuscript. (See pages 61 - 62)

THE BLUE ANCHOR 1898

Pages 394-395 in the manuscript. (See page 64)

H. F. VAN AND COMPANY LIMITED,

MANUFACTURERS OF ALL KINDS OF

AERATED BEVERAGES,

Lemonade, Ginger Beer, &c.,

MINERAL WATERS & CORDIALS.

ESTABLISHED 1875.

STEAM WORKS: BARKING & GRAYS, ESSEX

Page 399 in the manuscript. (See page 77)

Mr Brigley

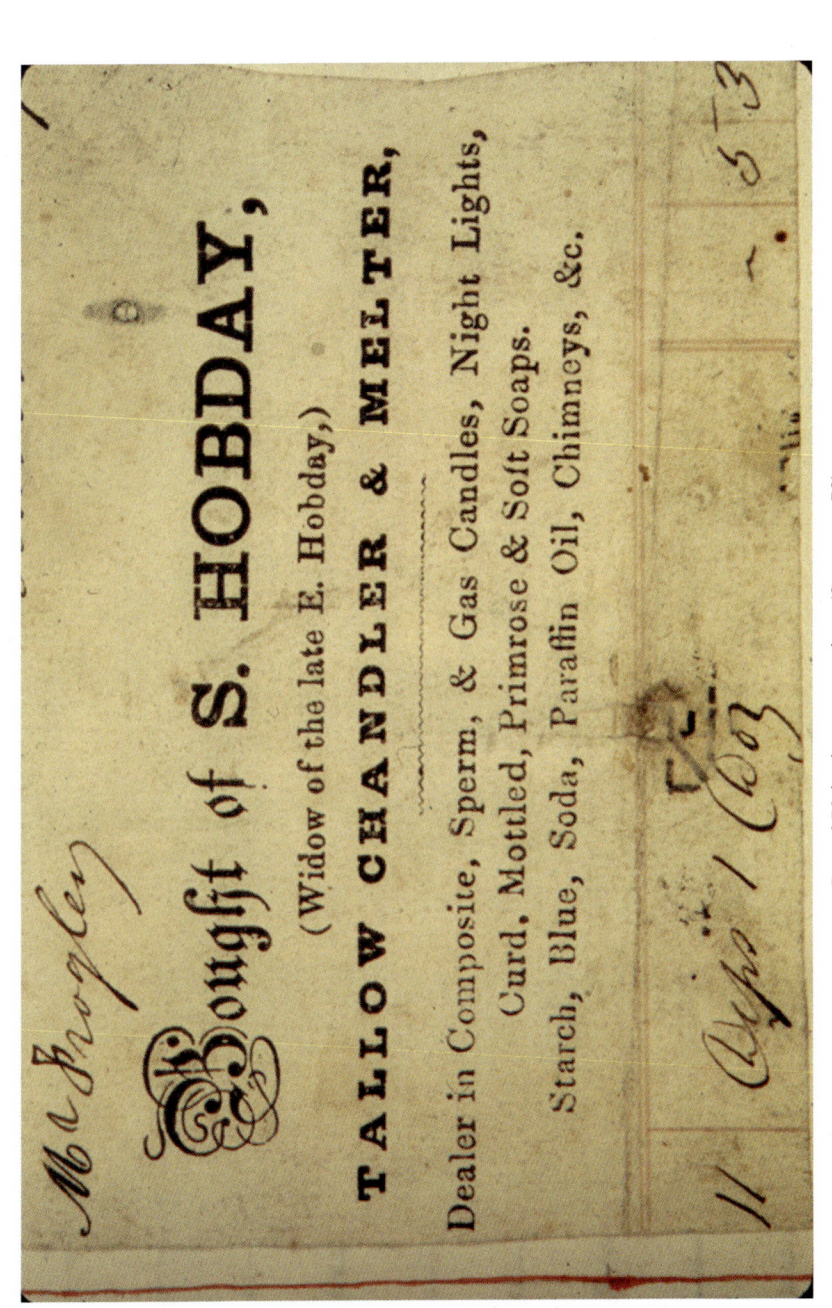

Bought of **S. HOBDAY,**
(Widow of the late E. Hobday,)
TALLOW CHANDLER & MELTER,

Dealer in Composite, Sperm, & Gas Candles, Night Lights, Curd, Mottled, Primrose & Soft Soaps, Starch, Blue, Soda, Paraffin Oil, Chimneys, &c.

Page 379 in the manuscript. (See page 79)

East Street in about 1925. (See page 108)

THE COCK BH in East St. - Frogley

Page 427 in the manuscript. (See page 109)

THE COCK PH, East st. c.1870

A rare photograph of the Cock, dated about 1870. (See page 109)

MR FROGLEY'S BARKING: A FIRST SELECTION

saw-pit. Dying in 1877 he was succeeded by his Foreman Mr Joseph Cooper & the business is now carried on by his son James.

The *Ship* [Page 396]

– evidently an old licenced house. "Christy" says in his book upon Tokens[122] that a William Martin of Barking Key[123] in 1688, issued some tokens with a ship depicted upon them. (These tokens were principally struck in the reign of Charles II, as from some cause (probably the civil wars). Small change was very scarce & the people themselves took the matter into their own hands, & issued copper peices known as "Tokens". They were often curious – many or most of them contained the name, occupation & address of the person issuing them. They were redeemable at the shops or the addresses on them & for the value placed on them. There was 359 specimens – or different tokens - issued in Essex – and out of which 11 was struck & issued in Barking).

Probably he [William Martin] had this Inn. Mr Thomas Linsdell[124] – who died in 1878 – was many years in this house. One of his sons James, was an Architect & Surveyor, but left Barking for Leytonstone. Henry Linsdell succeeded his Father in the business. He married a daughter of Robert Willett, Pawnbroker of Barking[125]. In 1874 great internal improvements was made by taking away the party walls & Mr C. J. Dawson carried the work out successfully, also in 188? external alterations was made. Mr H. Linsdell in July 1889 sold the business to Mr W. Hamblin of Grays[126]. Mr Linsdell left the Town & still (1910) resides near Forest-Gate. Mr Hamblin in 1892 sold it again to Mr H. Rowland & Mr Hamblin took the "Lamb" at Plaistow where he died soon after. In 1899 Mr Rowland sold the business to a Mr Allingham[127].

Anchor & Hope. This house is not in Heath Street but over the gates. From its position, with so many tributaries of the Roding about it, it suffered terribly by the Floods that once periodically visited Barking. In 1875 Mr John Smith (now a builder in Longbridge Road)[128] was landlord & the damage done to his stock

---

122 Christy, Miller *Trade signs of Essex*. Edmund Durrant, 1887.
123 Quay.
124 Thomas Linsdell, Ship, Heath Street; Eleanor Linsdell, grocer, Heath Street. (Pigot 1839); Thomas Linsdell, Park Cottage, Heath Street. (Kelly's 1874).
125 John Willett, pawnbroker, 22, 24 & 26 North Street. (Kelly's 1890).
126 William Hamblin, Ship P.H. & wine & spirit merchant, 32 Heath Street. (Kelly's 1890).
127 Arthur Woollett Allingham, Ship P.H., 32 Heath Street (Kelly's 1906).
128 John Smith, builder, Wishford House, Longbridge Road. (Kelly's 1890).

MR FROGLEY'S BARKING: A FIRST SELECTION

by a flood was £30. In a report of a valuation made at the time it said the cause was "on account of the walls & wharves not being at the height of the Standard Level as ordered by the Commissioners of Sewers". Mr John Smith was, I am informed, formerly a roadman or navvy & while here had under consideration a Scheme of Boring a Well to supply the town with water. In another flood in 1888 – when Mr Balaam was landlord[129] - the water rose to the top of the counter & he suffered damage to the extent of £100.

(The following account was given to me by an old inhabitant – a relative of mine - & I give it as I received it. "An old gentleman – a Smackowner of Barking - had been with some friends to the "Red Lion" in North Street and leaving there one dark winters night - & passing the Horse-Pond (that faced the old Abbey Wall) - he accidentally fell on the Ice, and laid there unconsious. A young man passing by a little later noticed the man laying on the Ice, & raising the old gentleman at once identified him & took him to his home. The old Gentleman on recovering conciousness and being told of this circumstances & considering the young man had saved his life, sent for him and promised that he would be a friend to him. The Old Gentleman kept his word, my informant confirmed, & through his benovolence the young man – Thomas Linsdell – was in a position to take the "Ship Inn". I have not attempted to verify this statement, but give it as I received it, as I cannot doubt the sincerity of my informant).

The Cutter – a small beer house near the shop, - closed up some years ago.

Hart-Street. [Page 397]

This street, runs by a curve from Heath Street to Fisher Street. Until recent times it contained few houses & which was occupied by Fishermens families.

Dorrells Foundry. Mr Dorrell[130] came to Barking in 1866 & commenced the business of a brass foundry in his kitchen, but eventually his business so increased that he was compelled to have a more suitable structure. Adjoining his house was a large shed – once used for boat building – this he hired, & a few years later he purchased a plot of land opposite & in 1880 he built here his foundry. It cost about £1000. Eventually however, chiefly through the life he was living, he lost the principal of his clients work. The writer always with others respected Mr Dorrell

---

129 John Baalham, beer retailer, West Bank. (Kelly's 1890, 1894).
130 Leo Francis Dorell, iron & brass founder, Phoenix Foundry, Hart Street. (Kelly's 1874, 1890).

MR FROGLEY'S BARKING: A FIRST SELECTION

& it is hard to try to pull the "mote"[131] out of anothers eye. But facts are stubborn. He got into difficulties – sold his interest in the Foundry & left the town with somebody elses wife & took a small Licensed house at Cambridge, where he lost all his money. In 1898 he was living at Manor-Park, having casual employment with his wife & family & died in 1900 very poor.

Southbury House – a good sized house tenanted some 40 years ago (1868) by the Misses Tuck[132] as a private School. Mr Moffatt also resided there. He was Manager to Messrs Hewetts & Co. and is noticed under North Street. Also it was the residence for years of Mr. James Linsdell, Surveyor &c. He also possessed a fine Bass voice & was one of the old choristers of Barking Church. Also Mr. Joseph Skinley[133] – once a captain of a Steam Carrier & later successor as the Manager to Messrs Hewetts & Co. (of Mr. Moffatt). Mr Joseph Skinley also took great interest in Local Matters & he was an ardent Baptist. He died here in 1895 & is buried in the Churchyard.

Gas Lane – a narrow thoroughfare leading along the wall of the Gas Works to a moderate sized brick house at the end of the lane. The house is called Park House & was the residence of Mr William Baxter, Smackowner[134]. Also Mr Alexander resided there, during the time he was Manager of the Jute Works.

Hart Street, similar to all the streets & roads in this immediate vicinity, was during the time of the Fishery Trade in Barking, a very respectable Street, but since the introduction of the various Factories here, the tone of this district – or spot – has passed through many viscisitudes & changed from a decent residential place to that of a slum.

Axe-Street. [Pages 398-400]

Axe Street is also an old thoroughfare, but I should imagine it to be a lane – or having the appearance of one - 150 years ago. The principal residence in it was Byfrons – in fact the only one worthy of notice. Byfrons contained about 13 acres – almost all of which comprised a park & large well kept

---

131 "Speck of sawdust" – *New English Bible,* Matthew, chapter 7, verse 3.
132 Misses Tuck, academy. (White 1863). According to the 1851 census, Mary Elizabeth Tuck was conducting a Ladies Seminary with her three eldest daughters (aged 16 to 22) as teachers and her two youngest (aged 9 and 10), together with three boarders, amongst the pupils. Later the eldest daughter, Emma, took over and by 1871 had transferred the school to the Clock House on Ilford Hill.
133 Joseph Skinley, Southbury House, Hart Street. (Kelly's 1890, 1895).
134 Samuel Baxter, smack owner, Heath Street. (Pigot 1839).

MR FROGLEY'S BARKING: A FIRST SELECTION

Orchard. The Old Mansion – described as a good house – was built by Dr John Bamber, an eminent & wealthy Physician of Mincing Lane, for his country house. He died in Nov 1753 & was buried in Barking Church. It next belonged to Sir Crispe Gascoyne[135], Lord Mayor of London, through his marriage with Margaret, daughter of Dr John Bamber. Sir Crispe G—— already possessed Westbury & other properties in Barking. He resided at Byfrons & died in December 1761 & was also buried in the old Church.

His son Bamber Gascoyne – who previously resided at No.10 Great Stanhope Street, London - succeeded his father to Byfrons & he came to reside here & his youngest brother – Joseph – resided at Westbury. In 1770 Bamber Gascoyne enlargened the house & improved it & also the grounds. He died in 1791 & his son Bamber succeeded, but resided at Liverpool. He was MP for Liverpool. Byfrons was at this time tenanted by an old family named Ibbotson. This Bamber G—— cut off the entail – which caused the house to be pulled down in 1808 & sold the site & Park[136] He died in 1824. The Park & Meadows attached was later tenanted by Lord Somerville[137] for his famous Merino sheep to feed upon. These sheep was introduced into this Country by him for the first time. Mr Edward Glenny eventually came into possession of this Estate & he built the last house that stood there. It was built in 1850. His son Mr Samuel Glenny[138] said that he always understood that "Tom Sayers" the pugilist worked on the building of this house & he lodged in a cottage close by. After Mr Glennys death, the House & grounds was sold in 1883 to a Mr Langston for £6000 & he sold the House to Mr H. F. Van[139], who pulled it down, and used the materials in the building of his mineral water factory.

In 1895 this Estate was mostly covered with houses & shops, & in that year the roads was made up, kerbed &c. The roads on this Estate are:- The Walk: Cook Street: Hardwick Street: Morley Road: Howards Road & part of Gascoigne Road.

135 Sir Crisp Gascoyne (1700-1761), Sheriff and Lord Mayor of London, Master of the Brewers' Company.
136 Frogley may be mistaken in thinking that the old Bifrons was demolished in 1808. The Cecil papers at Hatfield House include a letter from the solicitor Wasey Sterry to Bamber Gascoyne [2] dated 17 August 1815 which seems to imply that the house was still standing but advises him to sell the property. The park was offered for sale in September 1816, but in November 1817 Bamber Gascoyne agreed to pay Sir Charles Hulse, Lord of the Manor, £300 for having destroyed Bifrons without licence (Essex Record Office, Sage collection D/DSa 37).
137 John Southey Somerville, 15th Lord Somerville (1765-1819). *Dictionary of national biography*, vol.53, 1898, p.253.
138 Samuel Glenny (1845-1910).
139 Henry Van, refreshment rooms, 48 Heath Street. (Kelly's 1890, 1900).

MR FROGLEY'S BARKING: A FIRST SELECTION

In a Cottage [Page 399]

– now No. [ ] Axe Street – with a small builders yard attached, once resided Mr William Holmes, Bricklayer & Builder[140]. This esteemed man came to Barking early in the 19th century & starting on his own account, soon through his business habits & upright manner gained the confidence of the Gentry of Barking. He built the Gas-Works – Reform Place – Loxford Hall I believe & many more buildings still standing in Barking Parish. All his children was born in Barking – but now (1910) only one is living – Mrs S. Dawson of Wall-End. He died in 1866 & his devoted wife in 1867. He was grandfather to Mr C. J. Dawson, Surveyor of the Council ... .

"The Victoria" was held by Mr Binks in 1876 when he died & his wife Elizabeth sold it in 1882 & took the "Commercial" in East Street. The house is one of the few named after Queen Victoria - although she reigned so long. Since 1882 it has undergone great alterations – in fact almost rebuilt.

Whites Mineral Water Works[141]. These extensive works originated in the following manner: Mr H. F. Van, a son of Mr Van, late Chemist of North Street, was formerly employed at Beckton Gas Works, but in 1876 he opened a Coffee Shop opposite the Town Quay & corner of Heath Street & while there he made his own Mineral Waters & later worked up a good connection outside. He later took other premises in Heath Street known as the Wine-Stores to Manufacture Ginger Beer &c. His trade so increased, he acquired the land on the Byfrons Estate & built the Factory in Axe Street. He built his Factory by the assistance of some townspeople & it was considered the largest of its kind near London. The main building was 120 feet x 70 feet & was entirely covered by a slated roof on the Southern face & covered with glass having a Northern Aspect so as to admit as much light as possible without the glare of the sun, & it was so arranged that vans could pass in & unload their empties & then pass into the Stock room, reload & pass out of the Factory. Soon after its erection, for some reason, he formed a liability Company, but this appears to have been unsuccessful. I have no doubt, that Mr Vans misfortunes occurred through want of capital. It was eventually sold to Messrs White & Sons of Camberwell, who have greatly enlarged it & made many improvements.

---

140 The 1851 census shows that William Holmes, 60, Master Bricklayer employing four men, was born in Creake, Norfolk; his wife, Mary, 63, in Chatham, Kent. Their cottage in Axe Street would have adjoined Padnal Place.

141 R. White & Sons, mineral water manufacturers, St Ann's Road. (Kelly's 1890). Demolished in the winter of 1972/73.

MR FROGLEY'S BARKING: A FIRST SELECTION

Mr Van afterwards moved into a double fronted bricked house – called Park House – in front of the Works. He opened here public Baths, but was compelled to abandon the scheme. At Park House previously resided a Mr James, Lighterman. The iron Fence in front originally was in front of Laurel Cottage (later the Swan) Queens Road, Barking. Mr Van left the town and after trying various commission agencies decided to reside in Woolwich (Charlton) and in 1907 commenced again to manufacture Mineral Waters & the various hot drinks.

(Mr Van, Senior, Chemist, left Barking in 1891, after having carried on business there for over 20 years & on his leaving the Town was presented with a Testimonial by the townspeople. He immediately opened a business near Southampton & where at that time a large Railway Company removed their works from Wandsworth).

The *Meeting House of the Open Brethren*, [Page 400]

built by the late Mr Edward Glenny of Byfrons. It is a small brick building & has a burial ground in the rear, where several members of this body is buried. It is now used as a Sunday School. A short distance away, another & more suitable building was erected in 1884, through the instrumentality of Mr Edward Glenny Junior & where this body now hold their services. It is called "Park Hall"[142] & computed to hold 600 persons.

The Twine-Spinning ground is at the rear of Park Hall. There are some good sheds attached for this business. Mr Cutmore[143] carried on the business here for many years very successfully, and was able to built some Freehold houses in Linton Road & eventually retire. He died in 1885. He was a devoted member of the Congregationalists … & is buried in the old churchyard. His successor was Mr T. R. Schrier[144] who came from Poplar. He still carries it on.

---

142 Park Hall, Axe Street. (Kelly's 1900). The Axe Street meeting room of the Brethren was built in 1846. Park Hall was erected in 1884, and New Park Hall in 1931.(Booklet *New Park Hall centenary year 1846-1946*). There were 77 internments in the burial ground behind the old meeting house, the remains being removed to Rippleside Cemetery in 1972 (information from Miss Gwen Cooper).

143 Henry Cutmore, rope maker. (White 1863). James Cutmore, rope & twine maker, Axe Street. (Kelly's 1874); died 1885. *St Margaret's churchyard: register of graves*. 1930. p.212.

144 Thomas Robinson Schrier, rope maker, Axe Street. (Kelly's 1874), rope maker, East Street. (Kelly's 1890) ; Mrs Charlotte Schrier, rope maker, Grove Place, East Street. (Kelly's 1894, 1900). By 1911 Messrs Pegley Bros Ltd were the owners, but a part of the works was wanted by the Council for an electricity works extension (Barking UDC minutes, 1911-1912, p.324). The position of the rope walk can be seen on the Goad fire insurance plan for 1908 (Sheet T60).

MR FROGLEY'S BARKING: A FIRST SELECTION

The Candle industry. While in Axe Street it should be mentioned that it was here that tallow candles – or dips – were made, for some 40 years ago. That is, about 1860 scarcely a cottage had anything to lighten their rooms except Tallow candles, & in hot weather what a trouble it was to keep them upright in the Candlesticks. One was as usual deemed sufficient to give the light but the room was always in semi-darkness. Then there was the snuffing of the wicks & sometimes in doing so one would extinguish the light altogether. These candles was manufactured at the rear of an Oil shop – nearly opposite the George Inn. It was kept by Mr Hobday[145], and after his death his widow carried on the business. The man who made the dips was named Mr E. Mills[146], and after the death of Mr Hobday he succeeded to the business, but at this time … business – so far as these dips or tallow-candles was concerned - was fast dying out. The composite candle superseded them.

Previous to the year [Page 379] [147]

1839 the town was probably lighted by the dim old oil lamps or lanterns – or neither – and the Places of worship, Shops & houses depended for their light from Candles. The writer has purchased often candles from the shop (still standing) in Axe Street where these candles called "Dips" was made, & from which the whole district for miles was supplied. After the death of the proprietor Mr Edgar Hobday in 1864 the business was carried on by his widow Mrs Sarah Hobday until her death in 1876, during which time the candles was made by a man – Edward Mills – and who succeeded his mistress to the business, but by this time these particular candles, "Dips" or tallow-candles had nearly died out. As these candles constantly required "snuffing" every house then possessed a pair of snuffers, which today is considered a "relic" of the past, as both the "Dip" Candle & Snuffers has practically dissappeared & its rival – a still popular candle called "Composite" - has taken its place.

---

145 Algar Hobday, tallow chandler, Axe Street. (Pigot 1839, White 1848). Forename is given as Edgar in White 1863 and Elgar (d.1867) in *St Margaret's churchyard: register of graves*. 1930. p.153 and 1851 census. His wife Sarah Sewell Hobday died in 1876.

146 Edward Mills, tallow melter & oilman, 12 & 14 Axe Street. (Kelly's 1890); oil & colour merchant, 12 Axe Street. (Kelly's 1894, 1900).

147 This description of candlemaking introduces the section on Barking Gas Works on pages 379- 382 of the manuscript.

MR FROGLEY'S BARKING: A FIRST SELECTION

The *fishing industry of Barking*. [Pages 305-312]

For many years the "Fishery" was the staple industry of the town, but deep sea fishing apparently is not very ancient. Smiles says "The herring fishery commenced about 1787, although the Dutch fished there previously & sold in our markets". Originally fishing was chiefly confined to the rivers which abounded with fish, & the Thames was equal to any.

Beyond Creekmouth the water was salt at high tide & every variety of fish was caught there. Also the following facts prove that for many centuries Barking was a noted fishing town:

1320   Master John-le-Fishmonger & others produced at the Guildhall before the Lord Mayor 16 nets called "Kiddels" taken in the Thames while under the charge of Pelham le Fishmonger of Woolwich & another from Plumstead. These nets belonged to the men of Barking, Erith & Plumstead, who were charged with placing the nets there to the destruction of small fish & salmon. These nets were destroyed!

1349   John de Goldstone of Barking & two Greenwich fishermen was taken with 5 false nets and 3 bushels of fish too small for use. Being brought before the Lord Mayor they were remanded & it was ordered that the nets should be burnt – the men being sworn not to use such nets in future & to find sureties for their good behaviour. Two men Nicholas Clark & H. Barritt stood for Goldstone (G. Jackson[148]).

1405   Mr G. Jackson also relates an incident when about 2000, including (among others) Henry & John Pragill, William Olive & Thomas Squirrell of Barking attacked the Inspectors with bows & arrows to defend their nets. They also shot at the Officers who were in boats filled with armed men. The men were pursued to Barking where the Officers landed & delivered to the constables there, in the presence of Thomas & Stephen Inglefield, the 16 nets mentioned until the Mayor should cause them to be sent to be examined & adjudge them. But the fishermen came & took the nets from the constables, wherefore the Lord Mayor, Aldermen & Commonalty did pray the Kings Council to take the matter in hand; whereupon the Council

---

[148] George Jackson, librarian, Barking Public Library, East Street. (Kelly's 1900). He lived in Ivy Cottage, James Street.

MR FROGLEY'S BARKING: A FIRST SELECTION

commanded one of the Kings Serjeants of Arms to arrest the principal rioters, & Pragill, Olyve, Squirrell & John Martins – dwellers in Barking – with others – was brought before the Council at Westminster. The men were condemned & tendered their submissions. They were allowed to fish with their nets in conformity with the standard of London & that in future all nets should be examined by the Lord Mayor before being used.

1593   David Ingram[149] of Barking, mariner, sailed with "Hawkins" to America.

1605   Sir Nicholas Coote (November 9th) examined a fisherman at Barking named Richard Franklin & he reported that Henry Paris his master had transported Priests & goods to Calais, France, on behalf of Richard Fuller, alias Johnson (State papers). Henry Paris resided near Colchester & possessed boats, & Guy Fawkes (alias Johnson) hired a boat from him to carry another & himself from Barking disguised to Gravesend, & having done so they were brought back, but after the explosion their intention was to be conveyed to France.

1642   3 large whales came up the Thames – 1 was caught at Gravesend & another at Greenwich.

1646   John White, described as an Arch-Pirate, had his Estates at Barking, consisting of his dwelling house & land, sequestored by the County Committee. He however petitioned for their return & a Mrs Margaret Cordwainer, Widow of St Olaves, Southwark, said she purchased the House from White in 1646, & she leased it to him, at a yearly rental of £80. Although White said he lived peaceably as a Fisherman & had paid rent for 2 years, the house was seized in 1648.

1649   Two Barking vessels belonging to Gates Taylor & Edmund Bonson were rescued from the Irish by Captain Copping. The vessels was ordered to be appraised & their owners to give security to abide by the sentences of the Admiralty Court and then to have them back.

1653   John Hudson & Sam Charsley, fishermen of Barking, were impressed for the Service, also a John Wood, but a pettition was

---

149 "David Ingram of Barking, who sailed with John Hawkins to West Africa and the Caribbean in 1567-9". *VCH Essex*: vol.5, p.239.

MR FROGLEY'S BARKING: A FIRST SELECTION

presented for their release by the Rev William Ames Vicar here. These & others were at this time pressed to service in a vessel called a "Ketch" & named the "Nonsuch" - a quick vessel & built at Barking in 1653 & carried six guns & considered a very quiet sailer. The next year (1654) it was hired by the Navy Commissioners for the [?] Guard. At this time the same accounts (State papers) mentions other vessels built at Barking, and hired chiefly for purposes of arresting pirates.

1654 About 2000 bolts of reed were cut off the marshes near the "Creek" for the stores at Woolwich.

1655 Captain Walter Perry of Barking owned the "Endeavour" & this was hired at £180 a month – It carried 4 guns & was recommended by Vice Admiral Lawson for the Fleet, in the Downs & in which was other Barking Vessels. About this time & for a number of years, a Government Pinnacle "the Henrietta" was stationed at Barking, watching the fishermen & sometimes stoping them for oyster carrying- smuggling – forbidden trawls &c (Jackson).

1656 Also at this time there resided in Barking a representative of a noted Essex family called "Fitch"[150]. There were three branches of the family. Thomas Fitch resided at Barking – having married Agnes, daughter of John Wiseman of Canfield, Essex, also an influential family. Sir William Fitch of Barking (son of Thomas & Agnes) married Dorothy, daughter of Sir Charles Cornwallis & several of his children was Christened at Barking Church (eg: Anne, b.1612; Dorothy, b.1613; Francis, b.1616; Elizabeth, b.1620; Charles, b.1620; William, b.1627).

[Page 307]

Sir Williams name is remembered in a murder trial as follows:

"Felton, the murderer of the Duke of Buckingham, had lodgings for about 9 months in London & his Landlord was a Thomas Foot, a servant to the Lord Warden of the Fleet. Felton announced to his landlord that he was going to the house of Sir William Fitch at Barking. Foot & his wife were both examined on this affair by Sir John Finch, Attorney General to the Queen &

---

150 Painting of Fitch arms, pedigree and extracts from Barking parish registers 1612-32 are in the Sage collection at Essex Record Office.

MR FROGLEY'S BARKING: A FIRST SELECTION

Attorney General Heath". (Examination Sept 18, 1628).

The foregoing incidents only refer to the Fishermen of Barking – and not to the deep-sea fishery which will now be considered.

Deep sea fishing [Page 307]

was introduced to the port of Barking in the 17th century - & probably trawling – and in the 18th century welled smacks was introduced by the Harwichs fishermen & was later adopted by Barking fishermen, who it is said ingeniously improved upon it, and it was considered by other towns as a peculiar trawl. As this trawl continued in force a description will be given:

"The net used by Barking Fishermen – called a trawl – with a beam & irons, the beam was used to keep the mouth of the net open. The trawl scraped close to the bottom of the sea & drawn along by the vessel, the gear being of proportion to size & weight".

The object of the welled vessels was to preserve the fish alive – a kind of false bottom - & through which the salt water flowed where the fish was contained, but in later years as the fresh water gradually reached to Gravesend, the vessels transferred their fish – either to be sent by rail or by some smaller craft called "Hatch Boats" to Billingsgate. About the commencement of the 19th century the deep sea fishery was gradually developed by Mr Hewett & so rapidly did it grow that eventually it became the chief support of the town. Scrymgeour Hewett a young Scotchman came to reside at Barking, & if old inhabitants – fishermen – can be relied upon it was through his enterprise that Barking soon became known as a fishing centre, & mainly from their accounts I write the following interesting particulars.

Mr Scrymgeour Hewett[151] commenced with one vessel called the "Liberty" & soon added another called the "Increase". (After 40 years of good services rendered, the Liberty was broken up & the stern-rail placed in the garden of Fawley House - a small house on the site of the present one in East Street – where Mr Hewett resided).

---

151 Scrymgeour Hewett (1769-1850), who married Sarah Whennell (d.1811), the only daughter of Barking smackowner Thomas Whennell (d.1837) in about 1794. Well worth recording is Thomas's epitaph in St Margaret's churchyard which reads as follows:

"*His anchors cast, his nets declined,*
He died in peace with all mankind.
To Heaven above is gone, I trust,
And there to mingle with the just"

MR FROGLEY'S BARKING: A FIRST SELECTION

Still very successful, in a very short time he [Scrymgeour Hewett] added 3 more vessels in the following order: the "Flemming", "Matchless" & "Fifeshire"[152]. These vessels were from 40 to 50 tons burden & being constructed with wells, preserved the fish alive for the London Markets. He died in 1850 and was buried in his wifes grave who pre-deceased him in 1814. His son Samuel[153] succeeded him and by this time great strides had been made. The number of fishermen in 1850 equaled a fourth of the population of the Parish (Barking & Ripple). The population was 4930 – exclusive of 1213 fishermen away. The vessels which numbered some 150 were also larger & much improved. To this Samuel Hewett must be accredited the honour of not only improving his vessels ..., but about 1840 he not only introduced ice, but he manufactured it, & for that purpose erected an "Ice House" at Barking – being the first in this country.

(This ice manufacture [Page 308]

commenced a new industry in Barking. Singularly winters there were invariably more severe than at the present time. In 1838, so severe was the winter, that the vessels could not get up higher than Purfleet on account of the frozen state of the river. Farmers waggons was hired to convey the fish to London. Although not so severe the winters succeeding for many years was more "Arctic weather" than at present, hence, annually the marshes was flooded & soon covered with thick ice, & so long did it continue freezing that the marsh owners was well repaid by the skaters, who came from all directions. But the greatest source of profit to the marshowners, tradesmen & others was the sale of the ice to Hewetts Company.

All the marshes & ditches was cleared of its ice & conveyed in carts to the Ice House, where each load fetched from 3/- to 5/- according to size. During this time – some 20 years it lasted – during the winter time & certain weeks it was common to see a line of carts full of ice, reaching from the Barking Road to the Ice Houses in Fisher Street. The Ice House was burnt down in 1850, but soon rebuilt. Truly it can be said that Barking during that period was worth living in. I cannot remember any case of extreme poverty, there

---

152 The smack Fifeshire was pierced for guns and was used as a privateer. *The book of Barking*. 1931. p.46.

153 Samuel Hewett (1797-1871), who introduced the fleeting system and used natural ice to preserve fish.

MR FROGLEY'S BARKING: A FIRST SELECTION

seemed work for all & all was engaged summer or winter. There is no comparison so far as the general health – strength – comfort – contentment & social condition of the inhabitants was concerned that prevailed in 1860 & later with what prevails now in 1900. Everyone knew & assisted each other then – now I am afraid to express what I think.)

By this new enterprise the fish was packed in trunks at sea & preserved dead for the London Markets & continues so to this day. He [Samuel Hewett] was a born fisherman, having for 14 years previous to his fathers death been engaged on a vessel as Captain. He eventually turned the concern into a Company and afterwards retired to Yarmouth & where he died in 1871 – his wife Ann dying in 1841 - & both was buried in Barking church[154].

Mr Auckland, an old Barking inhabitant, but who later resided at Bishopsgate, wrote to the press in 1898: "I recall the Barking days of my youth as the happiest of my life. How fragrant was Heath & Fisher Streets with the smell of the pitch & tar – how well the stores was stocked with oil-skins, top-boots, Guernseys, red-caps, rope &c &c".

The above description although true & all old inhabitants can endorse, but it only gives a meagre picture of this portion of the town where sail-lofts, rope yards, boat builders, mast, block & trunk makers &c were found. In addition to all this was the fine old parks attached to Gentlemens Seats & as the increase of population only consisted of those issues from marriages contracted among the town folk, thus making it appear as though everyone was related to each other, the increase was not great, but as Mr Auckland continued in the letter mentioned above "these times have changed – and old associations disappeared, everything becoming new, but even the old state of things in Barking is preferable".

The Company – upon the death of Mr Samuel Hewett in 1871 – was & had been for some years managed by two of his sons, Samuel and Robert Hewett.

(Another brother [Page 309]

Flemming Hewett[155] went to reside at Gorleston, where he was also interested in some land. But he emigrated to Vancouvier, America[156] & died there Oct 1912.

---

154 Hewett entries in *St Margaret's churchyard: register of graves*. 1930. p.94-95.
155 Fleming Hewett, aged 52. 1881 census, Gorleston.
156 Presumably Vancouver, Canada.

MR FROGLEY'S BARKING: A FIRST SELECTION

Samuel Hewett, generally known as the salesman, had a residence at Tower-Hill (on the site of the present Coal Exchange). Coming to Barking each day in an old fashioned gig & grey horse, he would return again about 6 P.M.

Robert Hewett[157] residing in Barking, appears to have taken the most active part in the Company – he being Managing Director. His residence was Roding Lodge. He also was very active in local affairs – being one of the first members of the old Local Board & in 1889 was elected on the Essex County Council. About 1892 he retired from active business & went to reside at Bromley, Kent, & his son Robert Muirhead Hewett succeeeded, & he also continued to reside at Roden Lodge. Another son Graham Hewett[158] entered the legal profession & was appointed Vestry Clerk of Barking in 1890, but through his declining health resigned the same year.)

Messrs Hewetts fleet – called the Short Blue from its flag – during the sixties introduced steam-carriers (steamboats) to convey the fish from the vessels in the North Sea to Billingsgate. They possessed four. The first one was built at Barking & named the Lord Alfred Paget[159], after a Director of the Company & who often visited the town in his yacht. Once he was accompanied by the Prince Edward of Wales – who admired the well built, muscular fishermens wives.

The "Hallett", built at Stockholm in 1865 & 165 tons Register - foundered at sea.

"Wellesley", built 1865 – 132 tons Register. Lost at sea in 1893-4 & crew saved.

"Frost" was I believe the last built, but all about the same year.

Sometimes these carriers managed to do 2 journeys weekly, but mostly 3 journeys each fortnight. About 20 years afterwards an experiment was tried with them. They carried a trawl which they lowered & proved very successful, hence the sailing vessels was lengthened & converted into steam trawlers & some new vessels were also built at Barking. In addition to the Hewetts Company there were several owners of smacks in Barking, but there was four recognised fleets sailing from Barking & known by their different flags, but I believe all of them – the owners – emanated from Hewetts. These four fleets was Hewetts, Morgans, Forges & Reeds. Other owners generally owned & commanded one vessel & were also previously old captains of Hewetts vessels.

---

157 Robert Hewett (1826-1904).
158 Graham Hewett, solicitor & vestry clerk, 55 East Street. (Kelly's 1890).
159 Lord Alfred Henry Paget (1816-1888). *Dictionary of national biography*, vol.43, 1895, p.57.

MR FROGLEY'S BARKING: A FIRST SELECTION

(Although the fishermen of Barking [Page 311]

generally enjoyed prosperity, there were times when the small smackowners in their desire for success & leisure tried to exploit labour as the only way to achieve their ends & this was no doubt especially so in the Forties. It has been stated that the fish being brought as far as Gravesend was transferred to "Hatch Boats" & the vessels proceeded to sea again – thus often debarring a man from his home for several weeks. So in November 1844 the men met while at sea & eventually decided to strike for more time at home & a few other minor matters if their request was not granted without a strike. The masters did not agree to their wishes hence they brought their vessels home – to Creekmouth - & after staying idle a month, the Masters was compelled to agree to their demands & so the strike ended.)

Morgans Fleet, originated from James Morgan[160] who rose from a poor fisher boy to be a wealthy man – his fortune estimated to have been £80,000. His first vessel was the Sociable & in less than 7 years he possessed 10 vessels. He also purchased in Fisher Street a wharf – later called Morgans Wharf & Quay. He died in 1865. His Widow resided at Fawley House[161] – which she enlarged & improved – until 1892, when she left Barking for Sydenham & died there in 1895, aged 90. Old fishermen have asserted to me that the above £80,000 was obtained by sweating his employees & if so his widow lived to see much of this large fortune squandered by her sons. Her eldest son James became bankrupt after forming one or two companies, but they all failed. Their name is scarcely mentioned in Barking now.

(John Lester – a nephew of James Morgan Senr & to whom he was apprenticed – died in April 1906 at Barking aged 92. He became apprenticed in 1827 & before he was 21 became captain. Mrs Lester was able to retire many years before his death, but most of the old captains were pursuaded to speculate in a vessel –the same as a person would in a house with small

---

160 In the 1861 census James Thomas Morgan, 39, Smack owner and Fish salesman, is recorded as employing 100 men and 120 boys. He lived in Heath Street with his wife, Mary Ann, 3 young sons and 2 servants. Also living-in are 7 apprentices aged between 13 and 18, all from London parishes and probably poor law apprentices. A further 18 apprentices are accommodated in the house next door. Round the corner in Fisher Street lived his brother William Morgan, 36, Smack owner employing 36 men and 40 boys. His wife Mary, 4 servants and an apprentice sailmaker are resident. According to the list of records compiled by the Business Archives Council in 1981, Samuel Hewett bought the entire Gamecock fleet of 29 vessels in 1868 following the death of James Morgan.

161 Mrs Morgan, Fawley House, East Street. (Kelly's 1886, 1890).

MR FROGLEY'S BARKING: A FIRST SELECTION

capital – the vessel purchased from Mr Hewett or Morgan & most of the purchase money remained on mortgage. They found however that what with interest, cost of repairs, especially if they were damaged in a gale, & lastly but chiefly their inability to superintend the sale of their fish in the Market, hence large commissions &c &c, they were eventually compelled – if not lost at sea – to surrender their vessels in many cases).

In 1850 there was about 48 smackowners & many trades contingent to the fishery business.

Great anxiety reigned in Barking at the close of the Sixties, when it became known that the fishery trade would leave the town for good. The construction of the Great Eastern Railway it was said was chiefly responsible for this change. This Railway was extended to Yarmouth in 1867 & Grimsby also by the Great Northern, hence all the vessels were sent to those places & consequently there was an exodus of fishermen & their families. Although at the time other large industries came to the town the various wharfs & lofts &c, suitable only for a fishery trade, were closed up.

The last two vessels to leave the town – according to the writers memory – belonged to Mr John Quash & were named the William & Mary[162]. There is very little now in the town to remind us of the old fishing days, except the town quay & River Roding, and a very few inns such as the Fishing Smack, Jolly Fisherman, The Ship, Blue Anchor & Anchor & Hope.

Mr Mathews of East-Ham relates – among others – a story of the smuggling days. He said:- "Down to 1834-5 smuggling went at a great pace. Vessels brought goods up the Thames & they were often carted across the marshes. Two men actually retired out of this business. They kept agents at East Ham who twice a week brought a load from Barking Creek. On one occasion they were unable to get the kegs they had smuggled across the marshes – as the Excise Officers had heard of it – so they hid the kegs amongst the reeds & rushes. Some inhabitants heard of this & about 40 or 50 took jugs to the spot to obtain some of the contents, but they drank so much that they could not return home".

A few names of old Smackowners [Page 312] &c during the Fishery era:

d.1834 Read[163], James – relatives of the Forge family – resided in

---

162 This was, in fact, a single vessel - the "William and Mary" - built at Barking in 1856.
163 Reed.

Page 431 in the manuscript. (See page 112)

MR. ALDERMAN W. W. GLENNY, J.P.,

Page 429 in the manuscript. (See page 133)

THE PADDOCK - Frogley

Page 432 - 433 in the manuscript. Bert Lockwood has managed to remove any evidence of this being a "two-page spread." (See page 122)

THE PADDOCK - Corner of East Street & Ripple Road c.1900

Now the site of Boots the Chemists. (See page 122)

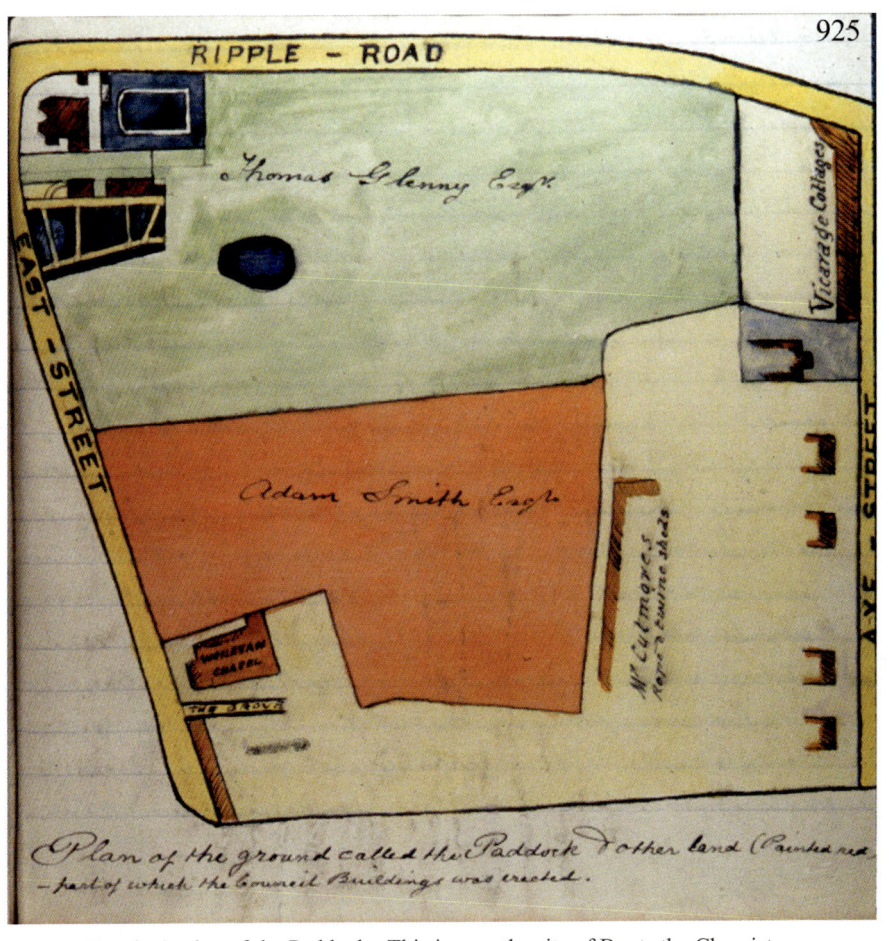

Frogley's plan of the Paddock. This is now the site of Boots the Chemists. Page 435 in the manuscript. (See page 122)

Gays Corner. 1676.

Page 434 in the manuscript. (See page 122)

RAILWAY TAVERN or PETO ARMS

Page 438 in the manuscript. (See page 123)

920

The new public offices, 1894. Page 441 in the manuscript. (See page 126)

MR FROGLEY'S BARKING: A FIRST SELECTION

Northbury House, North Street. Smackowner. The sons continued to reside there for many years.

d.1849 Grout, Joseph. Shipsmith & smackowner[164].

d.1849 Harris, John, resided in the Broadway. This was a large family in Barking & some were Smackowners – Sail-makers – Ship-chandlers - &c.

d.1855 Scrimes, John[165] – a ship & boat builder of Fisher Street.

d.1861 Forge, Richard[166], Smackowner whose daughter married a "Walrond"[167]. Also Thomas was his son, a watchmaker[168], died 1892 & John, died 1883, sailmaker and smackowner. This family is still represented in Barking[169].

d.1871 Horsley, William.[170] Mast, oar & block maker, Smackowner & Pump borer. His sister Mrs Ringer [171] died 1877 – previously kept the Still.

d.1856 Lake, John[172], resided in the Broadway. Smackowner, shoemaker & grocer. His son John died 1873, shoemaker in the Broadway & was the last "Beadle" of Barking Church[173] & his son William[174], shoemaker & later Rate Collector for the Local Board died 1895.

---

164 *St Margaret's churchyard: register of graves.* 1930. p.30:
"*A loving husband, a father dear,
An honest friend lies buried here,
Free from malice, void of pride,
So he lived and so he died*".
Joseph Grout, blacksmith. (Pigot 1839, White 1848). Family listed in East of London Family History Society: *1851 census index series: vol.1, pt.4: Barking.* 1984. p.16.

165 John Scrimes, blacksmith. (Pigot 1839). John Scrimes, shipwright. *St Margaret's churchyard: register of graves.* 1930. p.68.

166 *St Margaret's churchyard: register of graves.* 1930. p.30.

167 For Walronds see *St Margaret's churchyard: register of graves.* 1930. John Walrond, Overseer 1819. *Barking vestry minutes*, p.326.

168 Thomas Forge, watch maker & stationer, Broadway. (Kelly's 1874). For more details of the Forge family see Page 347 of the manuscript.

169 Thomas Forge, stationer & inspector of petroleum & clerk of the wharf, 27 Broadway. (Kelly's 1890).

170 *St Margaret's churchyard: register of graves.* 1930. p.51. East of London Family History Society: *1851 census index series: vol.1, pt.4: Barking.* 1984. p.19.

171 Rebecca Ringer. *St Margaret's churchyard: register of graves.* 1930. p.50.

172 John Lake, smack owner, High Street. (White's 1848)

173 John Lake, beadle, High Street. (Pigot 1839)

174 William Lake, house agent & collector to local board, Longbridge Road. (Kelly's 1890).

MR FROGLEY'S BARKING: A FIRST SELECTION

d.1872   Earle, Henry, Smackowner[175], resided in Station Road & later at Grimsby. His son Henry – once of the Still – boat builder & smackowner as was his father, died at Grimsby & buried their. His father was buried at the rear of Congregational Church.

d.1882   Marchant, Henry[176] – Smackowner – resided at "Northbury", Tanner Street. For many years however, he having sold his smacks, he became a salesman at Billingsgate. His wife Susan died 1889 & his only daughter & child Elizabeth in 1861.

d.1895   Marchant, William[177], brother of Henry, was also a smackowner, but retired for many years & resided in Axe Street. His wife predeceased him in 1877.

d.1881   Moffat, James, Manager to Messrs Hewetts. His wife Mary Ann died in 1882[178].

d.1902   Quash, John[179], of Northbury House, Smackowner – Originally a fisherman & afterwards Captain suddenly became possessed through a relative of some thousands of pounds. He purchased Northbury House & that is where his descendants still live. His wife Mary predeceased him in 1900.

d.1910   Harvey-George[180], Mr Harvey of 1 Jersey Road, Ilford. Died age 62 – son of Robert Harvey George, owner of considerable property in

---

175   Henry Earle, smack owner, Fisher Street. (White's 1863).

176   The 1841 census describes Henry Marchant as a Smackowner, then living with his wife, Susan, a servant and 4 apprentices in Vicarage Cottage, Axe Street. Sometime after 1848 he moved into East Street where he was living in the 1851 census, described as a Fish salesman. He was still there in 1866 (Kelly's) but then moved to Northbury House, Tanner Street, where he was living in 1874 (Kelly's). This house on the corner of Tanner Street and Harts Lane is easily confused with the Northbury House in North Street, which John Thomas Quash bought in 1867.

177   William Marchant, smack owner, Fisher Street. (White's 1863); 107 Axe Street. (Kelly's 1895). In the 1851 census and Kelly's 1855 and 1866, William Marchant, Smackowner, is shown living in Fisher Street. Later he appears under Private Residents in Vicarage Cottage, Axe Street (Kelly's 1874) – presumably the former residence of his brother Henry. It is called Vicarage Villa in 1886.

178   1892 according to *St Margaret's churchyard: register of graves*. 1930. p.196.

179   John T. Quash, 50 North Street. (Kelly's 1895). Died 1902. Quash family grave in *St Margaret's churchyard: register of graves*. 1930. p.207. Churchwarden 1870-81. *Barking vestry minutes*, p.324.

180   George Harvey, aged 33. 1881 census, Gorleston. George Harvey-George was the son of Robert Harvey-George of Ilford. He became manager for Messrs Hewett & Co at Gorleston

MR FROGLEY'S BARKING: A FIRST SELECTION

Barking & Ilford & who in 1878 managed the fishing business of Messrs Hewett & Co at Gorleston. The wife of Mr H. Harvey George was a daughter of the late Robert Hewett. He owns the Kingsfield Estate, Ilford.

[no date of death] Frogley, Joseph, retired fisherman, for 34 years Captain for Messrs Hewetts. Having property he resided latterly in his house Windsor Cottage, Longbridge Road – now the property of the Railway Company. His wife Jane, daughter of the late William Holmes of Axe Street Barking died [ ] & is the respected parents of the writer. They are interred in the cemetery[181].

The River Roding. [Pages 313-320]

This important Essex river, in its entire course covers a distance of about 37 miles long & the area it drains about 317 square miles. It rises at Brook-End near Easton & flows Southerly by many towns & villages. From North-Weald it flows south-west to Chigwell & Woodford – finally flowing south-east to Ilford, through Barking & empties itself into the Thames at Creeksmouth. The embankments is kept in repair by the owners of the adjacent lands principally, & the Hulse family – the owners of Barking Manor - is responsible for the greater part in Barking. Since 1875 the most of the walls has been considerably heightened – in some places 10 feet.

The portion of the River to be noticed here is from Creeksmouth to Ilford – a distance of about 3 miles – and along this portion has during the past 50 years been erected many factories.

Creeksmouth – the mouth of the River – has been noticed seperately, also the Southern Outfall opposite. From Creeksmouth the river to the Town-Quay is very zigzag & required great skills & judgement by those who navigated the Fishing vessels to & from the town. There was no danger, but it was common for a vessel to run ashore on the bends of the river – which often allowed the men to spend another day at home, waiting for a suitable tide to get them off. Along this route has sprung up several factories, but they have all been noticed on other pages.

---

and was a prominent member of the Yarmouth Town Council. He married a daughter of Robert Hewett and finally returned to Ilford. A prominent mason, he became Chancellor to the Province of England and was buried at Barking in full robes.

181 Joseph Frogley (1819-1902), fisherman and storekeeper, married Jane Holmes (1825-1901) in 1848. It is strange that Frogley leaves the dates of their deaths blank in the manuscript. Joseph was living at 44 Longbridge Road in 1895 (Kelly's). The house still exists.

MR FROGLEY'S BARKING: A FIRST SELECTION

We now arrive at the
Town Quay
said to be the largest Creek on the Thames & no doubt has always been the most important. A few centuries ago it was the principal traffic way to & from London as a few incidents will prove. Here Guy Fawkes (alias Johnson) hired a boat to convey him to Paris (see Fishery), also a great many vessels for the Navy was built here. The two first steamboats that plied between North & South Woolwich for the Great Eastern Railway was built here & named the "Essex" & "Kent". They were christened by the Lord Mayor of London & at the introduction of the Free Ferry they were replaced by more modern boats & finally broken up in 1894.

In Charles II reign large quantities of oak-trees were felled in the forests of Epping & Hainault & used for the building of the Navy. They were taken to this Quay & shipped to Woolwich. It should be noticed that in consequence of the great traffic to & from the Quay it was essential to keep the wharves in good repair hence tolls was enacted so that other districts using this wharf should contribute their share & the question of tolls has been a debateable point ever since. The following is an account of a meeting upon the question:

"At a Vestry meeting held in 1714 at the Church the following decision was passed. It is ordered that all persons making up to the Town-Wharf shall pay Wharfage & also that Mr Thomas Bennett (probably a relative of Capt Bennett who was buried at Barking in 1706 & a Benefactor) – present Churchwarden of Barking - do erect & put up a Turnpike or bar at the corner of Brickwall near the Crostree for Man-carts, carriages & wagons in order to oblige them to pay wharfage – except such carts as go to or from on any occassion   to the mills or to the hospital wharf or Granary".

In 1786 by an Act of Parliament certain duties & powers were conferred upon a body of persons called "Directors" for the maintainence of the quay & this system continued until 1889. Mr Ogbourne[182] writing about 1812 mentions that in that year (or about) the Quay was rebuilt at a cost of £690. During 1851 an animated scene was witnessed here. It was decided by the Government to dissafforest – mostly Hainault as it was estimated that it contained over 100,000 oak trees alone. These were sold to the Crown for £21,000. They were then carted to Barking & there was a continuous stream

---

182 In fact Elizabeth Ogborne, *The history of Essex from the earliest period to the present time*. Longman, 1814.

MR FROGLEY'S BARKING: A FIRST SELECTION

of these carts passing through the town. Later other woods were cleared & the land prepared for farming purposes at a cost of about £42,000, but I believe now most of this site is covered with bricks & mortar. In 1881 the Quay was put in repair at a cost of £100.

At the division in 1889 of the Parishes of Barking & Ilford, the powers conferred upon the Directors in 1786 was now vested in 5 Conservators – 3 of whom resided in Barking & 2 in Ilford parishes. They retired annually but could be re-elected at the Vestry, & both parishes conjointly were responsible for the maintainence of the Quay. For what reason I do not know, but in 1892 it was decided to hand over the control of the Quay to the Local Board. At this time there was much discontent in Barking respecting the increasing number of "Outsiders" using the Quay & an agitation arising was no doubt partly the cause of the Local Board taking over the control. According to statistics at that time – in 1891 – there were 197 barges unloaded for Outside districts & only 62 for Barking & Ilford. The Quay at this time was in a bad state of repair & it was estimated that quite £800 would be required for the work. In March 1892 the Conservators in their report said "The time is now come that the Wharves should be kept up at the expense of those using it by charging a Toll or fee for each barge".

A newly formed party in Barking called the "Progressives" strongly opposed the scheme & demanded a poll of the Town, which eventually took place and the following was the resulting votes:

For the scheme	534
Against the scheme	289
Majority in favor	245

Subsequently a Local Act was obtained placing the Quay absolutely under the control of the Local Board & by previous arrangement – if successful in obtaining the Act - the expenses was to be borne by Barking. In July 1894 a Mr Hocking of Stroud, Kent undertook to do the repairs then stipulated by the Board for £355 & in the following September a Mr F. White – who married into a Barking family – was appointed Wharfinger at 30 shillings weekly. I understand he was the first wharfinger of a permanent nature. In March 1895 the Board decided to make the Quay free again as there always appeared to be a loss.

Although the above resolution was passed the Quay was not free until 1896

MR FROGLEY'S BARKING: A FIRST SELECTION

& it remained so for one year – the Wharfinger still being employed. During that year 700 barges were unloaded & it was estimated that £230 had been forfeited by freeing the Quay, hence in May 1897 at a Council Meeting, it was decided to charge a toll on each barge not exceeding 50 tons register, & £1 for all steam & other vessels not included in that description for every 48 hours or part thereof.

During 1898 the number of Barges unloaded was 386 for the following districts: East-Ham 203: Ilford 163: Barking 20.

New Page & Calnans Wharf. This wharf during the fishery time was a boat & smack building yard & the site of their present offices was a cottage & a Smiths-shop attached, occupied by a family named Sullinge – but not for many years have they been represented in the town. About 1874 Mr Benjamin Glenny carried on the Wharf as a Builders Merchant, at which time he also contracted with Messrs Inde Coope, Brewers of Romford to bring their cargo (Barrells of Beer) to the Quay by traction engines. He was succeeded by Linnard & Sons, Coal Merchants[183], but they failed here. After others, Messrs Page, Calnan & Co became established here. They are large Builders Merchants & have yards at Plaistow & elsewhere.

The Water Mills [Page 316]

– or Abbey Floor Mills. There existed in Barking & on this spot Flour Mills nearly as ancient as the Abbey to which they belonged. This Mill was worked by water power. Domesday Book mentions a Mill at Barking & it was a possession of the Abbey & very valuable, as in Henry VIII time it was valued at £20 a year – a large rental for that period.

Early in the 18th century it [the mill] was held by Mr Robert Smith[184] who died in 1747. He was son of Robert Smith Esqr, Miller of Rotherhithe & Poplar The Flour Mills at Barking continued in this family until about 1816 when Mr Whitbourn[185] – of Leatherhead, Surrey - purchased them. At his

---

183 W.J. Linard & sons, seaborne coal & coke merchants, wharfingers & carmen, corn & forage contractors, Linards Steam Wharf, Fisher Street. (Kelly's 1894).

184 "In this vault are deposited the remains of Robert Smith, late of this place, miller... He was the son of Robert Smith of Rotherhithe and Poplar". *St Margaret's churchyard: register of graves*. 1930. p.65.

185 Sharp & Whitbourn, millers, Town Quay. (Pigot 1839). Francis William Whitbourn,

MR FROGLEY'S BARKING: A FIRST SELECTION

death he was succeeded by his two sons – one of whom in 1862 sold them to Messrs Ridley & Sons[186] whom I understand also possessed Woodford Flour Mills (also on the Roding). Messrs Ridley finally gave up Barking Mills in 1897 & they since have been closed. In 1905 (November) the plant &c was offered for sale by auction, but not sold. Among the list mentioned for sale was 20 pair of mill-stones: 4 sets of 2 roller mills: 12 Grain clearing & 4 dressing machines: wheat grinders &c &c.

Leaving the Town Quay is the next portion of the Roding, to Ilford. This portion, about 2 miles, was originally very narrow & its appearance was very different to what it is today. It was no doubt very shallow & probably resembled very much that portion immediately beyond Ilford. In 1730 (10 George II) An Act was obtained which stated, that the river was unpassable for any boat or vessel fit to carry any goods from Ilford to Barking. Later the various landowners adjoining the river agreed to give what land was required to widen the river & the work was carried out at the sole cost & charges by Joseph Goodman Esqr of Middlesex. Evidently much land was reclaimed & since then this portion also has been navigable for barges from Barking to Ilford ever since that time. In recent years many Factories & Wharves has opened up along this course – also an important Law Action respecting the right of way of the river wall was decided & will be noticed here.

Howards Chemical Works. [Page 317]

(This firm first came into existence with Mr Luke Howard & William Allen, becoming partners. Mr Howard commenced business at Plaistow in the chemical line & Mr Allen at Plough Court, City, Pharmacy line. In consequence of the great increase of business they dissolved & Mr Howard continued the Chemical business & which he removed to Stratford. In 1840 he resided at Chesterton-House, Balaam St, Plaistow, from which Chesterton & Howard Roads are no doubt named. This house later was the residence of Dr Kennedy & is now (1911) a Club. Mr Luke Howard died in 1864). Mr

---

Overseer 1821, Surveyor 1827-28 & 1846-51, Churchwarden 1828-58. *Barking vestry minutes*, p.326. See also Kenneth Farries: *Essex windmills, millers & millwrights*: vol.3. Skilton, 1984. p.29. The Whitbourn family is treated more fully on page 184 of the manuscript under Loxford. The family has been extensively researched by Mrs D. P. Wildbore and photocopies of her unpublished works can be seen at Valence House.

186 T.D. Ridley & Sons, millers (water & steam), Town Quay. (Kelly's 1890, 1900).

MR FROGLEY'S BARKING: A FIRST SELECTION

David Howard, a well known County Magnate[187], purchased in 1898 about 30 Acres of land at Uphall for the purpose of building a new factory. Included in the purchase was Lavender Mount & the old Farm-House (see Uphall). The Mount he decided to preserve on account of its associations. Mr Howard is himself an antiquarian. The new works is called Mount Works & the noble shaft is 187 feet high. It is rumoured that eventually he or his successor will entirely remove to Barking his works from Stratford, in fact, several departments has been removed to Barking. In digging for the foundations of these works several Roman remains were found.

Crows Factory. Near the above are already established some smaller factories. Near the Railway line is Messrs Crows Factory – originally started at Bromley-by-Bow. (Its site at Barking & adjoining land was known as Harts Marshes & is entered from the town by a narrow road called Harts Lane. The Hart family was & is Butchers at Barking. There were 3 marshes bounded by the Railway, the Roding, a portion of Harts Lane, & the Loxford Brook). In 1895 Messrs Crow purchased 15 acres of Marsh land & the Bromley Works transferred to Barking. Another factory situated at Creeksmouth & belonging to this family was also closed & transferred to Barking. The style of the firm is Thomas Crow & Sons, pitch & tar distillers. Near here on these Marshes is Johnsons factory.

Clarks Wharf. Adjoining Barking Road & the river, used for timber & other lumber. It has a river frontage of 248 feet & is 137 feet deep. Mr Clark[188] resides at the Off-licence opposite & he formerly had a timber yard in Fisher Street & North Street. During the construction of the Railway at Barking I am told most of their stores was landed at his wharf – from which Mr Clark did very well for himself.

By-fords Wharf. [Page 318]

This wharf is situated on the East bank & abutting on the Barking Road. Mr Byford Senior[189] formerly resided at Barking and did a large business – coke contractor – with Beckton Gas Works. Eventually he took Moody Wharf,

---

187 David Howard was grandson of Luke Howard (1722-1864), who founded "the first manufactory of chemicals to be established in Essex" at Plaistow in 1797. *VCH Essex*: vol.2, p.493-494. Frogley certainly would have had access to this history.

188 Charles Clark, lighterman, reed grower, shipbreaker, dealer in English oak, ship & other timber & manure, & beer retailer, New Road & opposite the Bull, North Street. (Kelly's 1890).

189 William Byford, lighterman & barge owner, North Street. (Pigot 1839, White 1848). See Byford entries in *St Margaret's churchyard: register of graves.* 1930. p.59. William's sons Edward William, William Joseph and Thomas all drowned in 1845. John Byford, builders' material dealer, New Road. (Kelly's 1886).

MR FROGLEY'S BARKING: A FIRST SELECTION

Poplar & was apparently very prosperous. He resided then in the Barking Road – near Rathbone Street – in a house, not large, which stood in its own grounds & was surrounded with trees in a large garden. It was demolished about 1879 & the site now is covered with houses The active part of the business has for many years been conducted by his eldest sons, under the style of John Byford & Sons. (John Byford died Sept 1911 at Westcliff-on-Sea & is buried in Barking Cemetery. In 1856 he went to live in the Victoria, Axe Street, & later Barking Road as above, Canning Town. His father had a Beer house in North Street, Barking. His name was William).

In 1893 the firm purchased of a Mr Bartholomew the above land & Mr Byford considered he purchased the river bank adjoining the land, and in making the Wharf utilised the bank also. Along this wall – or bank – was a pathway to Ilford – seldom used - & which he closed up, consequently an Action was brought by the Barking Council as they considered it was an ancient right of way. It was an important case, & the whole question was "wether it was & always had been a public right of way". The Action was fought in the Chancery Division on 25 July 1896 & the Court decided that the only right of way to Ilford direct was by the Ilford Lane.

The Case (briefly):

The Plaintiffs (District Council) said that the pathway would date back to the Romans, was one of antiquity & had been kept up since Henry VIII's time. The Bank was composed of earth with grass growing over it & all along the top was a foot-path 4 or 5 feet wide – since anyone could remember. (This Bank – in common with the other river walls – has been under the control of the Dagenham Commissioners (see Embankments) who employ a person called "Marsh Bailiff" whose duty it is to periodically walk the walls & examine all the sluices &c connected with the Walls. His report is then communicated to the Commissioners & he receives 20/-[190] for each walk. This position has been held for many years by a family named Carter – for three generations. The father of the present Bailiff was appointed in 1845 & he retired in 1865, being appointed Bailiff to the West-Ham Corporation (called the Level Commissioners, who about 1870 by Act of Parliament was severed from the Dagenham Commissioners) He died at Plaistow January 1907).

---

190 20 shillings (One pound).

MR FROGLEY'S BARKING: A FIRST SELECTION

The following is some of the witnesses in the case :-.

Mr C. J. Dawson – Council Surveyor – could remember the path about 40 years & had used it.

Mr W. Gibbard had also known & used the Wall upwards of 40 years.

Mr J. J. Quash [ditto] 64 years.

Mr G. Jackson [ditto] 45 years.

Messrs Byfords however proved that people had been prosecuted & fined for using the wall nearer to Ilford, but I believe the greatest evidence in their favor was that it never was continuous to Ilford in consequence of some small tributaries of the Roding which broke the wall & it was impossible at times – at high tides – to continue the walk to Ilford. The cost to the Council was upwards of £1000.

West-Bank, appears to be that portion of the river wall from the Town Quay to the Barking Road. An old wooden house here (now standing in the rear of four cottages built in 1874) was the residence of a family named Bauckham [191], boat builders. It is built on piles & had it not have been so would have been demolished by the frequent floods that once occurred at Barking.

These *floods*, [Page 319]
occassioned by the overflowing of the Roding, was very frequent in Barking & Ilford – the former especially. The writer has seen comparatively half of the town flooded & boats rowed in streets near the Quay, but happily such improvements have been made to the Walls & sluices &c that floods is a thing of the past. (On Sept 30th 1764 a great many floods occurred in Essex. On this night a large breach was made in the river (Roding) between the Thames & Barking – 26 yards in length - by which most of the marshes between Barking & Rainham was overflowed & to add to this two other breaches were made at Ripple Level, but these were soon stopped). In 1824 the flood was said to have been the largest known then. Communication with Barking & East-Ham was by boats. In 1848 breaches occurred in the wall near the Windmill & the marshes adjoining was all under water. In 1888 (August) was possibly the largest flood ever known in the district. This flood, seen daily by the writer, affected other districts for miles around. The following is a brief account of it:

---

191 There are Bauckham entries in *St Margaret's churchyard: register of graves*. 1930. See also East of London Family History Society: *1851 census series: vol.1, pt.4: Barking*. 1984. p.4.

MR FROGLEY'S BARKING: A FIRST SELECTION

This flood extended to Romford & Tilbury – in fact nearly the whole of South Essex was under water. Locally, from Barking to Ilford, the volume of water rushing over the walls resembled immense waterfalls & in consequence caused several large gaps in the walls. Near the railway bridge that crosses the Roding a barge floated through one of these gaps & rested eventually in a marsh about 400 yards from the river. It remained in the marsh for over 10 years. Between Barking & Wall End good business was done with horses & carts in conveying people from Barking to Wall End & vice-versa. The force of water one day – flowing from Ilford across the marshes to Barking – was so strong that a horse & cart conveying people to Wall-End was completely washed into the marshes from the Barking Road. The horse was drowned. The farmers were the greatest sufferers & whose loss was estimated at several thousand pounds.

On the second day the water began to subside & it was painful to see the distress inflicted in nearly every home in the vicinity of the Quay & Fisher Street. A very popular man, the Rev Vincent Smith, Curate in Charge of the Mission-Hall in Fisher Street – undertook to see the people was fed & provided for temporilly until their homes was rendered habitable. Also through the exertions of W.W. Glenny Esqr a Mansion House Fund was opened to help the local fund & a sum of £150 was raised. The Local Fund reached £50. The number of persons who were compelled to take shelter for the night was 103 adults & 83 children. When the water subsided their homes appeared more as a mass of mud & filth.

The cause of this flood was generally believed to have been caused by some stacks of hay, by some means floated down the river from Ilford way to Barking Quay & reaching the large sluice gate there adjoining the water-mills – so blocked the gates that it was impossible to open them & hence the commencement of the Flood. But no doubt on account of its dimensions there was some other cause. A Mr Warner had 15 acres of Hay washed away. In Oct 1889 an enquiry took place & the commissioners of Sewers decided at a cost of £2300 to re-construct the sluices of the 6 gates at the Town Quay & do everything possible to prevent the floods if possible.

In 1895 (February) real Arctic weather generally prevailed throughout the country. The Creek & River presented an appearance such as no living person had seen there before. From the Quay to the Thames the river was covered with Ice several feet thick & to avert a flood a passage had to be cut through the ice at the first bridge (Barking Road) to allow the water to pass. Some of the marshes however were flooded & they afforded a splendid opportunity for Skating – a sport the writer can well remember on these marshes, attracting skaters from districts miles away. On one occassion Messrs Hewetts had a yacht mounted on huge skates on these marshes – the wind causing it to sail on the ice.

South-Essex Water Works. [Page 320]

The Pumping Station was erected in 1897 near the Roding & is approached by a walk from the Barking Road. It was built by the Metropolitan Board of Works into which all the Water Companies is now merged.

Previous to 1867 – or about – the water supply of Barking was principally obtained from a fine well situated in a yard opposite the Town Quay. Also most landlords of property had pumps attached to their houses, but the water purchased from the Water-cartmen (half-penny per pail) was generally used for drinking purposes. The last man to hawk water in this way was named Smith & he lived in one of the old cottages in the Broadway opposite the "George Inn". These water carts was really a kind of trolley on two wheels with a large barrell on it – drawn by a donkey.

About 1867 the South Essex Water Company laid pipes from their works at Grays to Barking & also at the same time erected the Reservoir in Queens Road. The origination of the Company I am informed was caused in the following manner: The large Chalk Works at Grays are said to be of great age- & by digging to a great depth the chalk improves in quality. In the digging an abundance of water was discovered which was pumped up & discharged into the Thames. This process however became very expensive so it was decided to form a Water Company for the purpose of supplying water to the Town & eventually the Company took the above name.

East-Street [Pages 425-442]

East-Street probably takes its name from its Eastley direction from the Church. In ancient records it is spelt: "Eastrate" – as far back as the 15th century, but undoubtedly it is the oldest thoroughfare in the Town. It is commonly known by the inhabitants as "Bull Street". It extends from the Bull Inn to the Railway Bridge, and so far as its appearance is concerned, it has undergone more changes than any street in the Town. So, as recently as 30 years ago (that is 1870) it was a very quiet thoroughfare comprising mostly

MR FROGLEY'S BARKING: A FIRST SELECTION

private houses & Market Gardens. The Bull Inn is on the corner & has been described with North Street, also some old property adjoining – of which the rough sketch will give an idea of the appearance of this position. I made the sketch on the day they commenced to demolish them. On the left is a portion of the "Bull" stabling. As stated the Title Deeds of this land date back to the year 1435 and formerly belonged to the Abbey. The sketch shows the Butchers shop which was pulled down with the old shops – No 5-7 & 9 East St & No 1 to 5 Morgans Court & Crooks Court at the rear in March 1906.

The *Duke of York*. [Pages 426-427]

Originally the sign of this house was the "Cock". In 1846 – before it was a licenced house – the Baptists by the Bishop of Londons Licence engaged a room here for their first assembly in Barking & continued there 4 years. It was a wooden structure mostly, and in its latter days was in a very delapidated state & was the only licenced house in the town that the writer remembered was entered by descending a few steps. It was one of those Inns in Barking mentioned by "Mayhew"[192] who says in his account of the poor of London that a tramp informed him there were in Barking 4 Inns that slept 46 lodgers of the tramp class. The writer in 1870[193] saw in the upper rooms, 4 beds in each room, and was informed that for many years that was the principal source of income to the house. In 1886 it was purchased from a Mr Clark by George Blaizley & in 1890 it was sold for £60. In 1891, in consequence of its unsafe condition – especially the rear part – that portion was repaired, but in [ ] it was demolished & the present house built upon its site, and re-named the Duke of York[194].

A little further on is No. 24 East Street – a moderate side[195] brick built house – once a marine store dealers tenanted by a Mr Crow & later a boys school kept by a Mr Cox, who also possessed property in Queens Road, Barking. He resided & died recently at a house in Queens Road, Upton-Park. It was next occupied by the Local Board as their temporary offices & is still owned by the Council.

---

192 Henry Mayhew *London labour and the London poor*. Various editions.
193 Probably the year in which William Holmes Frogley became a grocer's apprentice.
194 According to a newspaper cutting in the possession of Miss Gwen Cooper dated May 1967 (when the Duke of York was about to be demolished), Mann's brewery held deeds which stated the Cock to have been built in 1789. It was still called the Cock in the 1891 census when it had 13 lodgers.
195 Sized?

MR FROGLEY'S BARKING: A FIRST SELECTION

Near this house was a small old fashioned Bakers shop occupied by Mr Thomas Claringbold[196]. (He died in 1860 & was buried in Barking Churchyard – also his widow who died in 1890. Mrs Claringbold for many years during her widowhood resided at the house at the corner of the Church path. Her son was a chorister at the Church). The house & shop stood in its own grounds & in the rear was plenty of fine trees. On this land now stands houses & called:

The Grove. These old wooden buildings was demolished in 1887 & the present shops afterwards erected together with the 28 houses now called the Grove. In 1896 the Town Council decided to purchase the 28 houses for £4500, so that the Local Fire Brigade could all reside there, but the Local Government Board would not consent to it. I am however informed that the Council succeeded in their scheme.

Abbey Lodge is a long moderate sized bricked house of one storey. On its site originally stood a butchers shop & sheds, occupied by Mr David Death[197] whose son was recently an Inspector of Police at Forest-Gate. The shop and premises being demolished the present house was erected for Dr Davison [198] & who resided here for many years. In 1874 Dr Mason[199] came to reside here in succession to Dr Parsons who succeeded Dr Davison.

The Rose beer house (originally the Red Cow) is near the Abbey Lodge. It was a small house, entered by ascending a few steps. I am informed that a few years ago a certain "Benjamin Green" was tenant of this house & he was also a Well-borer. He died at Plaistow in January 1888 aged 99 years & was

---

196 East of London Family History Society: *1851 census index series: vol.1, pt.4: Barking*. 1984. p.8.
197 David Death, butcher, Bull Street. (Pigot 1839, White 1848).
198 Presumably Frederick Montgomerie Davidson, M.D. and surgeon. (White 1863).
199 Hugh Herbert Mason, surgeon & certifying factory surgeon & medical officer & public vaccinator No.3 District Romford Union, Abbey Lodge, East Street. (Kelly's 1890). In 1894, Doctors Mason, Huntsman and Swindells were running the Barking and East Ham Provident dispensary in The Broadway, which "was established to enable the working classes to ensure for themselves and their families medical advice during illness, by making small periodical payments". (Kelly's 1894). Mason & Perkins, surgeons, 21 & 23 East Street. (Kelly's 1900).Churchwarden 1885-88. *Barking vestry minutes*, p.322. Mason was the first Chairman of Barking Urban District Council in 1895. His wife was the first woman to be elected a town councillor in Barking and amongst the first in the UK. On the Masons' political importance, see H.H. Lockwood, *Barking 100 years ago* (1990) and Scott Baker, *Party politics and the people: the municipal politics of Barking 1894-1931* (University of Cambridge, Final year dissertation, 1995-6).

MR FROGLEY'S BARKING: A FIRST SELECTION

buried in West Ham Cemetery. Later for many years Joseph Arrow[200] – a native of Barking – was tenant. He was a nephew of Mr Henry Earle who at one time resided at Barking. Residing for many years at Grimsby he eventually died there & Joseph Arrow – his nephew – benefitting by his Estate - purchased the Rose. In 1889 he sold it as a surrender for the Westbury Arms in the Ripple Road. The sign of the "Rose" is very uncommon in Essex says Mr Hatton – certainly there is one less now.

Fawley House [Page 428]

– I call this a moderate sized, but handsome residence, & it was built on the site of a smaller house by the late Mr James Morgan & occupied by Mr Samuel Hewett[201]. (Mr Morgan purchased the house from Mr Hewett, correction). Mr Morgan rose from being a Fisher-boy to possess a fortune of £80,000. He died in 1865 aged 40 & was succeeded by his Widow Mary Ann, who resided here until 1892 when she finally left Barking & went to Sydenham, where she died in March 1895 & was buried in her husbands tomb in Barking Churchyard[202]. Mrs Morgan possessed other property in the town, but sold all of it in 1892 – Mr Thomas Pelling, Grocer &c of North Street purchasing Fawley House[203], where he now resides. The house is double fronted with very large stone Bay-windows & porch entrance. It contains 9 bed-rooms: Dining room: Drawing-room: Bathroom: Kitchen: Wash-house &c. Adjoining the house is a spacious & ornamental Conservatory, Stables & excellent Garden, in which stood for many years the figure-head of the first vessel Mr Morgan possessed. I believe it has dissappeared for many years.

The White House[204] – a medium sized house painted white. It stood in its own grounds – had a good garden & plenty of fine trees. Dr Manley[205] – an

---

200 Joseph Arrow, beer retailer, 9 East Street. (Kelly's 1890); 13 East Street. (Kelly's 1900).
201 Scrymgeour Hewett bought the site from Alexander Glenny in 1822 (Manor Court rolls) and lived there until his death in 1850, followed by his younger son Thomas, who died in 1861.
202 Entry in *St Margaret's churchyard: register of graves*. 1930. p.165.
203 Thomas Pelling, grocer & agent for W. & A. Gilbey, wine & spirit merchants, 21 Broadway, & grocer & baker, 27 Heath Street, & 79 High Street, Plaistow. (Kelly's 1890); 21 East Street. (Kelly's 1895).
204 The house was demolished in November 1899 and replaced by the London and South Western Bank (note on Essex Record Office copy of Sage sale catalogue no.31).
205 John Manley, Bull Street. (Pigot 1839). "Sacred to the memory of Annie, wife of John Manley, M.D. of Westbury House". *St Margaret's churchyard: register of graves*. 1930. p.236. Overseer 1834-36 and Churchwarden 1843-58. *Barking vestry minutes*, p.322. John Manley, M.D., Westbury. (White 1848).

MR FROGLEY'S BARKING: A FIRST SELECTION

old resident of Barking - resided here previous to taking Westbury House. The last tenant I believe was Mr Benjamin Glenny – a builders Merchant & brother to Mr William Wallis Glenny. Mr B. Glenny leaving Barking about 1900 it was pulled down in 1901 & the present bank erected on its site. This Bank – the first Commercial Bank established in Barking – had their premises a few years previously in East Street opposite the Bull Inn yard.

Previously to 1888 the paths was very narrow in East Street, similar to what is to be seen in any country village, but in 1888 they were widened & tar-paved. The writer recollects that nearly all the Paths in the town – including North Street – was very narrow, without any kerb-stones. In this condition they had remained for a number of years, but since the adoption of the Local Board, such is the alterations taken place in the Town, that an inhabitant who left the town 30 years ago would scarcely recognise it to-day.

Cecil-House, [Pages 429-431]

the residence of Mr William Wallis Glenny JP[206] &c, is a large modern brick building standing in its own grounds about 200 feet from the roadway, and is surrounded by a large garden. Adjoining the garden & seperated by a fence is the farm-yard – some Barns & Stabling. In 1894 (March) Mr W. W. Glenny retired from farming and his live-stock, farming implements &c was then sold by Auction[207].

Mr William Wallis Glenny is a descendent of an old Barking family engaged in the agricultural industry. His parents was Mr Thomas and Mrs Harriett Glenny[208]. (Thomas Glenny died 20th January 1861 & was buried in Barking Churchyard. Harriett his wife survived him many years, dying 24th February 1876 & was buried in the City of London Cemetery, Ilford). W. W. Glenny, as was most of the family, was a member of the "Plymouth Brethren". After the death of Mrs Harriett Glenny he continued to reside at "Cecil House"[209] & does so to the present time. In addition to the Farming business, he took great interest, & became an active worker in local & eventually in County

---

206 William Wallis Glenny (1839-1933) had 208 acres at Barking. In 1879 his farm won second prize in a competition designed to encourage farmers in the London area to grow more vegetables. (*Farmers weekly*, 24 August 1973).

207 In 1895 William Wallis Glenny contributed an article "The onion and its cultivation" to the Journal of the Royal Agricultural Society (p.257-275).

208 Mrs H. Glenny. (White 1848).

209 A modern brick building demolished in 1936.

Dove-House Estate

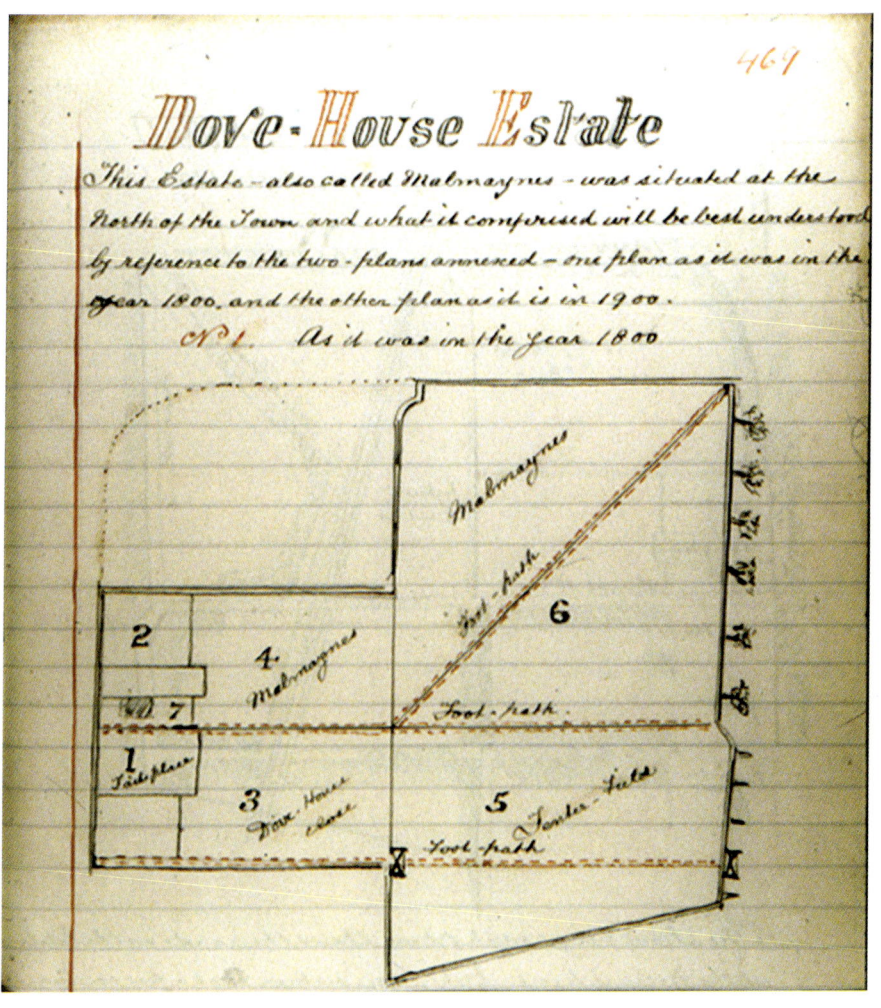

This Estate — also called Malmaynes — was situated at the North of the Town and what it comprised will be best understood by reference to the two plans annexed — one plan as it was in the year 1800, and the other plan as it is in 1900.

Nº 1. As it was in the year 1800.

Page 469 in the manuscript. (See page 146)

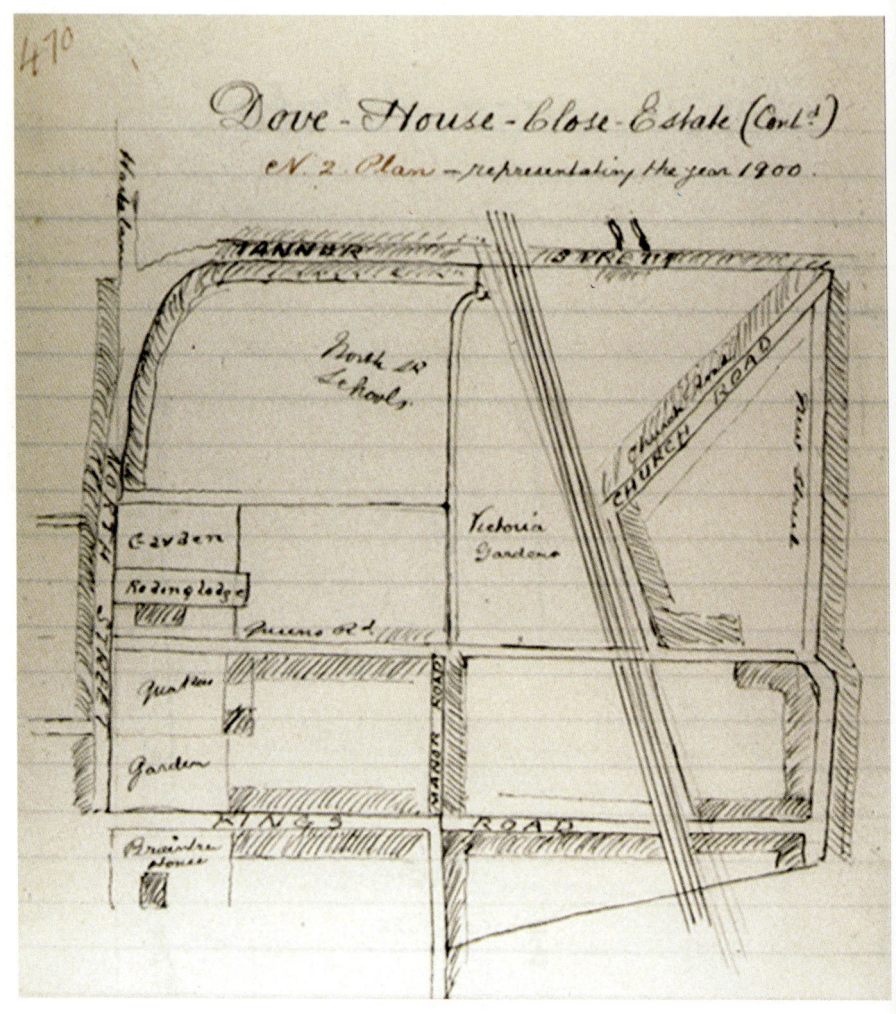

Page 470 in the manuscript. (See page 147)

Page 331 in the manuscript. (See page 146)

LAUREL COTTAGE c.1871
alias the SWAN B.H.
The Frogley family once lived next door in Ivy Cottage

Page 473 in the manuscript. (See page 149)

HOUSE IN TANNER STREET

Page 478 in the manuscript. (See page 153)

TANNER STREET

MOULTRIES
GENERAL STORES
Tea Coffee & Provisions
Best & Cheapest

966

J. LOUTHS HOUSE

Page 480 in the manuscript. (See page 153)

OLD SHOPS IN EAST STREET 1906 - Frogley

Page 425 in the manuscript. (See page 109)

119

Page 478 in the manuscript. (See page 153)

MR FROGLEY'S BARKING: A FIRST SELECTION

matters & was a staunch Conservative. From 1868 to 1879 he was Surveyor for the Town of Barking & about 1878 was appointed Magistrate to the Beacontree

[Page 430]

Division of Essex. Also in 1888 he was elected to represent Barking on the Essex County Council, in 1889 he was elected Alderman on the Essex County Council and in 1892 he was elected Vice-Chairman of that body. He has also acted as Chairman of the Romford Board of Guardians, the Barking School Board & the Local Library Committee. Singularly he was a Candidate of the First Election of the newly formed Local Board but was not successful, & he never offered himself again. Of the Barking Charities he is an old Trustee.

As I stated he retired from Farming in 1894, and after the sale the stables abutting on to East Street was converted into lock up sheds. Mr Glenny is well informed in Parish and County matters & his great knowledge of historical matters & important events that have happened & taken place in this ancient Parish would be invaluable to the historian. He is a most genial man, always happy to advise the poorest of his townspeople. As an Employer he was most respected, and a great many of his men regretted when he retired from business. The writer – in common with many more – sincerely hopes that Mr W. Glenny will be spared many years yet, and continue to live amongst them at Cecil-House. He is certainly the chief among his own family and of the Town also & by the old inhabitants no man has been or is even now more respected – for they know him. Of all the old influential families that resided & had large interests in Barking, the Glenny family only remains in the person of Mr William Wallis Glenny.

The Glenny Family.

I regret I am unable at present to give an history – or enlarged account - of this family, especially as it is still represented in the Town, but on another page I will give information gathered from Burials &c, including my own personal recollections. The latter will of course chiefly refer to the representatives of the Family who have resided in the Town since 1870. I hope to be in a position at a future date to have a fuller account of this family, who have been during the past century, connected with the affairs of the whole Parish.

MR FROGLEY'S BARKING: A FIRST SELECTION

The *Paddock*[210]. [Pages 432-435]

The house & land is situated at the corner of Ripple Road & East Street. The house was built in the "Georgian" style, probably by Mr Roger Vaughan who I am informed possessed it – early in the 18th century. Mr Vaughan died in 1756[211] at Barking & was a Brandy Merchant. One of his descendants also resided here – Mr Joseph Bladsworth[212] - & he died about 1812 & was buried at old East-Ham Churchyard. Later it was occupied by Mr Whitbourn[213], brother & partner of Francis Whitbourn Esqr of Loxford. The house, double fronted, brick, & tiled roof with all out buildings, together with about [3.5] acres of land attached was purchased by Mr Thomas Glenny[214], Brewer for £2500. Mr T. Glenny retired from active business in August 1907, leaving the management of the Brewery to his nephew George, son of William Wallis Glenny. The house was demolished in December 1907 & large handsome business premises has been erected on its site, & a new Police Station on a portion of the land.

Gays Corner. [Page 436]

This portion of East Street is situated at the corner of East Street and Station Road. It is now occupied by shops, but the site was previously in the occupation of a Mr Gay, Market Gardener[215]. There was two small cottages, an ordinary farm yard & stables. Mr Gay had 3 sons, and they are now successful farmers at Dagenham & Chadwell-Heath. I have called this "Gays Corner" to identify the spot, but the Gay family is not an old Barking family.

Proceeeding on this side of East Street to the Railway there is not much to notice, but as, in consequence of the recent Railway improvement at this spot, some properties are demolished, I will mention them. After leaving

---

210 In about 1911, Councillor Arthur Blake built a furnishers and ironmongers on this site, which became known as Blake's Corner. Its distinctive clock tower was demolished following bomb damage in 1941. Boots the Chemist now occupies the site.

211 *St Margaret's churchyard: register of graves.* 1930. p.22.

212 J. Bladsworth, Barking Overseer and Surveyor 1787 and Churchwarden 1790-1791. *Barking vestry minutes*, p.318.

213 William F. Whitbourn, farmer, Loxford Hall. (White 1848). The Paddock was put up for sale in 1882, following the death of Henry Whitbourn (information from Mrs D.P. Wildbore).

214 Thomas Glenny (1842-1914).

215 Joseph Gay, market gardener, 21 Cambridge Road. (Kelly's 1890); William John Gay, farmer, 43 East Street. (Kelly's 1894).

MR FROGLEY'S BARKING: A FIRST SELECTION

"Gays Farm Yard" there was a few small houses built by & belonging to Mr Henry Seabrook of the "Fishing Smack", Fisher Street. At the corner shop of Cambridge Road Mr Samuel Glenny commenced his business as a Auctioneer. Continuing was a few shops, of modern date.

The Railway Tavern – or Peto Arms. This house was erected in 1850 and named after Sir Samuel Morton Peto, one of the contractors for the London, Tilbury & Southend Railway[216]. In 1855 a Mr Jessie Bailey[217] took the house & carried on the Business for 26 years – he died there in March 1881[218] and his widow continued there until August 1882, when it was purchased by Mr Joseph Tracey[219]. Mr Tracey was a well known man in the district, and during his tenancy several clubs – quoits &c – was started here. He sold it in 1897 to a Mr Lewis[220] – who I beleive was the last tenant previous to closing it. During Mr Baileys tenancy there was very few alterations. The Bar was small & had tap-rooms, but Mr Tracey thoroughly altered the internal arrangements, & also improved the external portion by adding several entrances to the house. In consequence of the Railway improvement the House is now closed – a considerable amount was paid as compensation – and now the fabric is a wreck. After Mrs Bailey left the above House, she I am informed took the Golden Fleece, Forest Gate. In 1902 the writer saw her & her daughters at Broadstairs, where they kept the "Crown". Mrs Bailey died there in 1904 and was buried in St Peters Churchyard, near Broadstairs. The Daughters continued the business at Broadstairs. They were much respected & some Barking folks often visited them.

The *Alms-Houses*. [Page 437]

All the houses between the Railway Hotel and the Ripple Road – in East Street - was demolished on the south side except the Almshouses for the Railway improvement. According to Mr "Morant"[221] there was three houses in Bull Street (East Street) and two in the Ripple road but the donors was

---

216 Sir Samuel Morton Peto (1809-1889). *Dictionary of national biography*, vol.45, 1896, p.86-88.
217 Jesse Bailey, Peto Arms, East Street. (Kelly's 1874).
218 *St Margaret's churchyard: register of graves.* 1930. p.154.
219 Joseph M. Tracey, Peto Arms P.H., East Street. (Kelly's 1890).
220 James Oliver Lewis, Railway Hotel, East Street. (Kelly's 1900).
221 Philip Morant *The history and antiquities of the County of Essex, compiled from the best and most ancient historians.* 2 vols. T. Osborne, 1768 & 2nd edition, 1816.

MR FROGLEY'S BARKING: A FIRST SELECTION

unknown. It seems curious that the Benefactors now cannot be traced, but it is most probable that at a very early date some Benefactor cared for the poor of Barking in this direction. The first Almshouses on record was founded by a William Elsing Esq, Mercer, in 1332, when he endowed a House for the support of a hundred blind men, & a John Stodie who in 1358 built & endowed a house to support 100 poor citizens. Others soon followed their examples, and as so many of the most wealthy of London Merchants resided in Barking Parish, one of them at an early date may have built some at Barking. In 1614 Mr John Wylde or Wilde – a resident of Barking Parish - bequeathed two or three cottages in East-Street to be used as Almshouses for the Poor[222]. Another authority – trustworthy – says it was one house only, containing four rooms, but it is evident that Mr Wylde left several.

(There was a family named Wilde residing in this Parish for many years. In 1595 Mr Edward Wilde resided at the Bee-Hive, Ilford. The above Benefactor Mr John Wilde resided at Barking, and a John Wilde – probably his son – left lands in Edmonton for the purpose of apprenticing two boys to a trade and also to support three Almshouses & other charitable purposes in 1662. I have been informed, but have not verified it at present, that John Wilde was a printer of Stationers Hall & Aldersgate Street and that one of his apprentices (in 1706) was Samuel Richardson[223], the celebrated printer to whom Goldsmith came as printers reader. This is reported in Lloyds News of November 30th 1908, & I was informed that the "John Wilde" was from the Barking family).

The present Almshouses was erected in 1861, and in 1879 the cottages (2 or 3) mentioned above in East Street was purchased by Mr William Lake for £225. These cottages was situated at the rear of Mr Lakes shop, which was on the corner of East Street & the Broadway. By the sale of these cottages, two more houses was added to the seven built in 1861. The houses have four rooms each & accommodate 21 inmates. In consequence of the Railway improvement, a letter was received in December 1906 from the Charity

---

[222] For a discussion of this benefactor see *Essex Journal*, 1975, vol.10, no.4, p.129-133: "St Lawrence Spittel, Barking Abbey and the forgotten benefactor, John Wilde" by Kenneth Glenny. Also the latter's article "The forgotten benefactor" in *Barking Record*, 1976, no.92, p.7-12. Bert Lockwood deals with the complex problem of Wilde and the Barking almshouses in *Essex Journal*, Spring 1995 (vol.30, no.1), p.16-19 – "Barking almshouses reconsidered".

[223] The novelist Samuel Richardson (1689-1761) may have been born in Dagenham. In his will, he left lands, tenements and real estate near Dagenham to friends and relatives. *Dagenham digest*, no.44.

MR FROGLEY'S BARKING: A FIRST SELECTION

Commissioners to the Local Trustees, intimating that they agreed to the proposal of the Trustees to demolish the whole or part of the houses for the widening of this part of the railway. At a Council Meeting held the same month it was decided to draw a Cheque for £250 in favor of the Local Trustees. At this time it was almost decided to demolish the 9 houses & build new houses in another part of the Town near the Victoria Gardens[224], but eventually the two houses immediately facing East Street was demolished & in 1907 two more built at the rear of the seven.

Adjoining the Almshouses was some more cottages & in one of them resided for many years Mr John Jaggers the Local Carrier[225]. After he left Barking it became the office of Mr George Lamb[226], Surveyor, son of Ex-Serjeant Lamb of the Police at Barking. These cottages was demolished. Next was a cottage occupied by a shoemaker (or repairer) and then a cottage with the ground floor converted into a General stores. The whole of these cottages had a wooden fence in front, about 6 feet from the houses, but for some years the fences had been removed & small shop-fronts put to the cottages. The one above mentioned – General Stores – was brought out to the path-way and occupied by Mr [ ] Garland[227], formerly an employee at the Jute Factory. He was very prosperous in this shop. In March 1907 Mr Garland was paid £1250 by the Council as his interest – evidently he had a lease. Adjoining was a double fronted cottage, at one time occupied by Mr Albon[228] who had a Blacksmith shop adjoining. For about 15 years Mr C.J. Dawson, Surveyor to the Council[229], had his office there & he was paid £250 for his rights. The Freeholder of these two cottages last mentioned was Mr Thomas Pelling, Grocer[230], of Fawley House, East Street, and he received £2550 for the Freehold. These cottages were then demolished – the road widened and the present Bank premises built on the site of them.

---

224 Victoria Gardens, Queen's Road. (Kelly's 1900).
225 John Jaggers, carrier, East Street. (Kelly's 1874). East of London Family History Society: *1851 census index series: vol.1, pt.4: Barking.* 1984. p.19.
226 George Lamb, architect & surveyor, Norway House, Longbridge Road. (Kelly's 1890).
227 John William Garland, shopkeeper, East Street. (Kelly's 1890); fruiterer & greengrocer, 8 Broadway & 72 East Street. (Kelly's 1894); Private resident, 1 & 3 Hurstbourne Gardens. (Kelly's 1920).
228 Samuel Albon, blacksmith, 76 East Street. (Kelly's 1890, 1900). He died in 1893. His epitaph reads *"Whiter than snow"*. *St Margaret's churchyard: register of graves.* 1930. p.167.
229 Charles James Dawson, F.R.I.B.A., architect & surveyor, 70 East Street. (Kelly's 1900).
230 Thomas Pelling, grocer, 27 Heath Street. (Kelly's 1900).

MR FROGLEY'S BARKING: A FIRST SELECTION

Passing again the Paddock, where I understand the handsome new business premises now being erected for Mr Councillor Blake as a "Universal Provider" will soon be opened, is a peice of land (or was) previously used for Market Garden purposes. It measured about 190 feet frontage to East Street & contained about two[?] acres. This land was purchased by Mr Adam Smith, landlord of the Abbey Arms, Barking Road about 1886-7 for £1500 and shortly after he sold a portion of it to the Council to build their

Public Offices upon. [Pages 439-442]

As regards this sale I have my own opinion as to wether certain persons connected with the Council officially, did really act in the interests of the Ratepayers, or did they so conduct it that it turned out to be a very profitable transaction for themselves. Personally I detest casting reflections upon any one, especially without a decided proof, but I believe that if I could see the Minutes of the Council for some two years previous to the sale I should be justified in my suspicions.

For some time there was an agitation in the Town, for suitable Offices wherein could be grouped the various governing bodies of the Town, as previously the various bodies was compelled to hold their meetings anywhere, where it was convenient to find suitable premises or rooms. In the election of 1888 (Local Board) this agitation was very marked, but nothing – except buying the land – was practically done until July 1891, when plans was submitted by the Surveyor and finally adopted. The Local Government Board was asked to hold an enquiry – which was done – and in the following October it was decided to obtain a Loan of about £13000, to cover the building of the Public Offices – Fire Station – Library &c &c. The above enquiry was held in March 1892 when the following loans was submitted for consideration & the buildings the loans was required for.

Estimated amount for cost of the Public Offices about £6019

Estimated amount for cost of the Library portion about £2977

Estimated amount for cost of the Fire-Station about £1354

Estimated amount for cost of the Mortuary about £568

Estimated amount for cost of the Stabling, Sheds &c & paving & gates about £1260

MR FROGLEY'S BARKING: A FIRST SELECTION

Estimated amount for cost of the Formans Cottages & Walls about £376

Estimated amount for making a 40 foot road £2807 and other improvements £2807

Other improvements were included at a cost of about £2139

Making a grand total of £17500

The consent of the Local Government Board was not received until the early part of 1893 & in April the Tender of Messrs Dr Ayley & Co of Oxford Street London was accepted for the erection of the Public-Offices, Library &c, for the sum of £12,738 and the foundation stone was laid by Mr Thomas Wallis Glenny in October 1893. The only persons present was the Boards Members, Officials & their friends. Underneath the stone was deposited a current copy of the Times, Essex Times & the Barking & East Ham Advertiser together with three silver coins of 1893. The above Tender of £12,738 was for building only, as the cost of Fittings, Furnishings & some alterations constituted a further Loans, thus the following items was sanctioned by the Local Government Board in March 1895:

Cost (Estimated) for alterations & additions of the various offices ... £823

Ditto Library ... £380

Ditto Mortuary ... £32

Ditto Fire Station ... £101

Ditto Cartsheds ... £67

Ditto Foremans Cottages ... £15

Cost of Furnishing & Fittings of Public Offices £568

Ditto Library £355

Ditto Stables £3.15.0

Ditto Foremans Cottage £2.5.0

Cost of Buildings as for contract stated above £12738.0.0

Total £15085.0.0

The following is a description of the various buildings mentioned above except the Fire Brigade which is mentioned under Fire Brigade:

The front portion & the return fronts is faced with red pressed bricks from

MR FROGLEY'S BARKING: A FIRST SELECTION

the High Broom Company's fields at Tunbridge Wells, largely releived with Monks Park stone, richly moulded & carved. The roof is covered with Westmoreland Green Rag Slates – the ridging being of lead with bossed shell ornament on same & the whole surmounted by a Turret containing a Striking Clock with 3 illuminating dials. The deep rich red of the bricks, the mellow tone of the stone & the green slates of the roof forms a pleasing peice of colouring. The stone mullioned windows is fitted with metal casements made by the Crittal Company of Braintree and is glazed below the transomes with plate glass & above that with leaded lights of antique glass of a geometrical design. A wide open area on two fronts affords ample light & ventilation to the basement floor. The Plan of the Building consists of a central block with a wing on each side. The ground floor to the wing to the left forms the Lending & Reference Library & the first floor of the same forms the general reading room. This room is 49 feet x 23 feet x 16 feet high.

The basement floor of this wing & the second floor of the whole building (which is entirely constructed in the roof space) forms the Technical Class Rooms, the entrance to which is by the staircase wing to the extreme left. The remainder of the building forms the Boards Offices. The Basement contains a Drawing Office & Plan room, Caretakers Room and Apartments, Strong room, heating chamber, stores &c. The Ground Floor contains grand entrance hall & vestibule, large general office & Surveyors, Collectors Sanitary officers rooms respectively. The First Floor contains the Board room which is 49 feet x 23 x 16 feet high, an ante and Committee room & spacious landing. An inner lobby fitted with glazed oak screen & folding doors at both ends leads to the principal staircase. This is one of the principal features of the building: The stone chairs – 9 feet high – is fitted with moulded & carved oak banisters & handrail, & is divided off from the entrance hall & first floor landing by oak columns. The walls of the entrance hall, staircase & landing is lined to a height of 6 feet with embossed glazed tiles of an old gold colour. The floors is paved with marble mosaic & the ceilings is pannelled out with mouldings of geometrical design, the whole being lighted by stone-mullioned windows glazed with leaded lights.

The Board Room, which is really the chief room of the Building, has a very handsome appearance. The walls is lined with oak pannelled dado 6 feet 4 inches high & the ceiling is richly moulded & pannelled, suspended from which is 4 handsome iron gargeliers. The large oriel window & a similar

MR FROGLEY'S BARKING: A FIRST SELECTION

window on the return front gives a very bold and very pleasing interior effect. The fire-places are of moulded & carved oak filled with dove marble slips & glazed tiled cheeks & hearths. The building throughout is lighted with incandescent lamps ...

The Public Offices was opened on October 18th 1894 by Mr Passmore Edwards who was presented for the purpose with a silver key enclosed in a Morroco case. The Company present – admitted by ticket – was numerous. A Guard of Honour was composed of the Barking Fire Brigade and the Ambulance Corps. East Street was decorated its whole length. At the Luncheon that later followed, about 150 sat down, after which a grand concert was given.

The *Public Baths*. [Page 442]

In 1898 an enquiry was held at the Public Offices, to consider an application made by the Council to borrow £8250 for the erection of the above Baths. The Baths was later erected on land belonging to the Council, at the rear of the Public Offices. The building contains a swimming bath with pond 90 feet by 30 feet, dressing boxes &c, Womens & mens slipper baths, waiting rooms, Club rooms, Laundry, caretakers & stores departments consisting of Scullery, bedroom & sitting room. The slipper baths is enamelled porcelain. The Laundry is provided with a small engine & washing machines &c. Messrs F. Coxheads (of Leytonstone) tender of £7686 was accepted for the buildings, & including £1100 for engineering work & other costs the total cost was about £8500. In addition the shaft cost £200.

The Mortuary. (The old mortuary still stands at the North-West-Corner of the Parish Churchyard. It was originally built for a tool shed in a very out of the way place, & how it was that this shed was turned into a Mortuary is one of those problems one cannot understand). The new Mortuary is also situated at the rear of the Public Offices & consists of a shell store & two chambers for bodies – each holding two – one chamber being used for infectious cases, the walls of which are lined with white glazed tiles. Running the whole length of these is a viewing lobby, hermetically sealed from the Chambers & fitted with viewing windows of plate glass on metal sashes, the walls of which are lined with brown glazed tiles. At one end of the viewing lobby is a clothes store, properly lighted, ventilated & fitted with plate glass doors. This will be used for displaying the wearing apparell of dead bodies that have not been identified at the time of burial. The external face of the walls are faced with

MR FROGLEY'S BARKING: A FIRST SELECTION

Luton Blue bricks, releived with Blue Staffordshire brick plinths & stone dressings. The roof is covered with plain red tiles.

The Postal Services of Barking. [Page 455]

Originally – that is until recent years – the Post Office was situated in Axe Street – opposite the George Inn, at a Grocers shop kept by a Mr Stevens[231] for many years. He had two daughters and a son[232] who assisted him, & who also carried it on after their fathers death. The letters was collected from Barking & conveyed by a small cart – painted red – to Ilford. The last man who drove this cart was named Webster. Often this "Cart" was stopped in Ilford Lane but the practice of sending to Ilford was discontinued in the early seventies (I believe about 1876) and Mr Webster then became Landlord of the "King Harry" beer house in North Street. Eventually an agitation came about as the accommodation was inadequate with the increasing population. In 1890 the Local Board memoralised the Post Master General on the matter & accordingly a sub-office was opened in Tanner Street at Mr Moultries[233] Grocers shop in 1891. In 1892 another sub-office was opened at a Dairy shop near the Station in East Street, kept by a Mr Kirkman[234], but the want was not supplied, so in 1895 new and suitable premises was taken in East Street, near the Wesleyan Chapel and a Mr Webber[235] appointed post-master.

The Fire Brigade. [Pages 366-368]

The headquarters of the Fire Brigade was originally at the old Townhall. About the year 1834 Barking Town was presented by the authorities of the Royal Exchange with a fire engine – one of the old fashioned manuals – provided the town kept it in repair. The first captain was a Mr Pearson, and he was succeeded by Mr Sibley, a plumber, but the engine was neglected and was in a bad state of repair. In 1875 the "Lighting Inspectors", a newly

---

231 William Henry Stephens, grocer, oilman, glass cutter and postmaster. (White 1848); grocer, ironmonger & post office, Axe Street. (Kelly's 1874). Alfred Stephens, postmaster, 6 Axe Street. (Kelly's 1890, 1894).

232 Alfred Stephens, distributor of stamps, address given as "Pavement". (Kelly's 1890).

233 John Moultrie, grocer, 31 Broadway & Tanner Street. (Kelly's 1886, 1890); draper, 17 Tanner Street. (Kelly's 1894); sub-post office, 17 Tanner Street. (Kelly's 1900).

234 Benjamin Kirkman & Sons, dairy & post office, 79 East Street. (Kelly's 1894); William & Alfred Kirkman, dairy & post office, 120 & 123 East Street. (Kelly's 1900).

235 Thomas J.F. Webber, postmaster, Axe Street. (Kelly's 1900).

MR FROGLEY'S BARKING: A FIRST SELECTION

formed body of townsmen, had the engine examined and repaired, also extra hose was purchased – and standposts erected, the Hydrants taken over from the Water Company.

About this time there was several fires, but the Fire arrangements appeared absolutely useless. Sometimes the time from when the alarm was given, and the men started with the engine, was so long that the writer has seen people return from the fire – then burnt out – and meeting the firemen, told them the fire was out. The difficulty was to find the firemen, who worked at Ilford, Beckton and other places. Also to get the horse has delayed the men a considerable time. If the fire was in the town, it was more common to see the engine drawn by 30 or more boys with a long rope. Mr T. Forge was Captain at this time (he was appointed in 1870) and the writer once saw the boys drawing the engine, but when they got to the fire Mr Forge could not stop them running away with the engine until they had traversed a few streets.

In 1879 a better system was adopted. The Lighting Committee was enabled to purchase a new engine with the money saved by lighting the town with Oil since 1875. Also in 1879 a Mr Sidney Hill was made Captain. He had been a Naval man, but unfortunately his leg was broken in 1882 and he was compelled to resign. He was succeeded by Mr John J. Quash, a young man & native of Barking. I do not remember that he had any previous experience of the kind, but during his Office the Brigade rose to its present efficiency. His ambition was to raise the Barking Brigade, at any rate equal to any other Volunteer Fire Brigade, and in this I believe he succeeded.

In 1884 a grand competition took place (on August 21) in the "Paddock", East Street, open to any Fire Brigade in the County. Prizes were competed for, & although Barking missed the 1st Prize it was not far behind. In March 1891 each Firemens life was insured. The Captain for £250 at death or permanent disablement – and if injured temporally £1.10.0 a week during illness. 14 Firemen at £100 each at death or permanent disablement or temporary £1 a week. In November (1891) uniforms was supplied at a cost of £40. In 1895 more hydrants were fixed & Hose & other necessaries was purchased at a cost of £150.

The following year (1896) the Council decided to purchase the cottages in the Grove, East Street for Firemens dwellings, but the Local Government Board would not sanction it. The price agreed for the cottages was £4500. In December 1896 the Town Council took over the control of the Brigade and each fireman was to have a retainer of £1 a year and 2/6 for each drill: the

MR FROGLEY'S BARKING: A FIRST SELECTION

Captain £26 a year and 3/6 each drill. Some of the members had put in several years of service, so at a concert held at the Spotted Dog in May 1897 they received long service medals. The following were the recipients:-

Capt J. J. Quash[236]	15 years service
Lieut J. Malvin[237]	15 years service
Lieut R. Newman[238]	15 years service
1st Engineer F. Wagstaff[239]	15 years service
2nd Engineer J. Brown[240]	10 years service
Fireman W. Vesey[241]	10 years service

In the following January 1898, the Council purchased a Steam Engine and accessories at a cost of £322. It is capable of discharging 300 gallons per minute. They also possessed then one 6 inch manual – Hose Cart – a 45 lattice Girder Escape with shoot, and a portable ladder escape. The Brigade numbered 14 members, and in August 1898 the National Telephone Company connected 10 of their dwellings with the Police Station by means of bells, to the Fire Station.

The new Fire-Station is situated at the rear of the Public Offices in East Street, and was opened conjointly in October 1894, but the Fire Station alone was formally opened on the New Years Eve 1894-5. It is a smart building and up to date. It contains the usual offices, Firemens quarters &c. The front is faced with pressed bricks relieved with stone dressings, and the roof is covered with plain red tiles. There is also a Hose tower, which is finished with a bossed lead perforated ridge and terminals. In the rear is a two horse box stables with tower. In Feburary 1905 the Captain, J. J. Quash, resigned the position, and Mr George Gallager – Engineer to the Sheffield Fire Brigade - was appointed at a Salary of £100 per annum.

Glenny family. [Pages 465-466]

This an old & respicted Barking family – of which in the town resided many good families, but the Glenny family alone now is represented in the Town.

---

236 John James Quash, hosier & glover, 10 North Street. (Kelly's 1886).
237 James Malvin, 79 North Street.
238 Robert Newman, 12 Bamford Place.
239 Frank Wagstaff, 3 Cambridge Road.
240 John Brown, 4 Garden Place.
241 Lived at 4 Northbury Cottages, North Street.

MR FROGLEY'S BARKING: A FIRST SELECTION

When they first came here, or where they originated from I am not informed at present but for generations past they have mostly been successful Farmers [242]. In 1799 Mrs Deborah Glenny – probably a widow – possessed a Farm in the town. There was also a William Glenny who married a Miss Molly Sibley of Barking. They had other relatives here, viz Elizabeth died 1828 Age 67: Sarah, died 1838 Age 62: George died 1839 age 67: Alexander died 1843 age 78: William died 1850 age 81, and Mary (Miss) died 1856 Age 83 – all brothers & sisters of the said William. Mary, wife of William (1850) died in 1861 aged 83.

Thomas Glenny died 20 January 1861; he was husband of Harriett who died 24th February 1876. Harriett was buried in Ilford Cemetery, & previously resided in the "Great House" East Street. They were the parents of the following:

William Wallis Glenny – who succeeded his Mother in the Farms. He is a Magistrate and Vice Chairman of the Essex County Council. In 1882 he was defeated at the first Local Board Election. He is a Trustee of the Barking General Charities. In 1894 he retired from the farming business & sold off his plant. In 1889 he was elected on the new School Board & in 1891 elected on the Committee of Techinical Instruction. He was Surveyor of the Town previous to 1879 when his brother Thomas succeeded him.

Thomas Wallis Glenny – Brewer[243]. He was also a Surveyor of the Town under the old authority: 1889-1893 Local Board Member & became their chairman. He purchased the Paddock in [ ] & resided there. First elected on the Local Board in 1882 & retired in 1884. In 1892 he was appointed their Chairman & was defeated

---

242 The first record of the Glenny family in Barking is an entry in the Rate Book for September-December 1759 showing that Alexander Glenny was rated at £15 for Cobb Hall. This was a farmhouse built probably in the early 18th century on or near the site of a "great house" called Wakering Place alias Coblers Hall erected in the reign of Elizabeth I by William Nutbrowne but pulled down between 1653 and 1680. Alexander Glenny (c.1726-1782) had married Deborah Harison at St Mary's Islington on 7th October 1759. According to family tradition he was a farmer/market gardener from Scotland. They had 8 surviving children, and Deborah lived until 1804. The eldest child, John, started farming in Battersea; the second son, Alexander (1765-1843) was blinded in childhood and became organist at St Margaret's. William (1766-1850) and George (1772-1839), who remained single, farmed Cobb Hall. The freehold was bought in 1799, a new house built, and Bifrons estate bought from Gascoyne in 1816. William's son Thomas (1805-1861) inherited, followed by his eldest son William Wallis Glenny (1839-1923), who, being local Conservative leader, renamed the Hall, Cecil House. Edward (1801-1881), William's second son, inherited Bifrons in 1850. (Based on a lecture by Kenneth Glenny to Ilford Historical Society in October 1976).

243 Thomas W. Glenny, brewer, 18 Linton Road. (Kelly's 1900).

in 1894 at the first District Council Election, but later was elected & became their Chairman. He recently retired from business, leaving the managership with his nephew & leaving the town. He now resides at Sidcup, Kent.

George Wallis Glenny – was a partner in the Brewery business, but later entered the medical profession. For many years he has been a Missionary & recently died in that capacity. Occassionally he returned from South Africa to Barking, & preached here. About 1876 he became a Missionary & was in South Africa in 1906 but died shortly after. (I am informed he died on board a ship in 1909).

Benjamin W. Glenny[244], entered the commercial line – opening a wharf on the Town Quay as a Builders Merchant & Contractor. He resided in the White House, East Street but for many years has left the town for Colchester about 1900.

Harry Glenny at an early age left the town for America, where he became a Bank Manager. He died in 1904 leaving it was said some £3000 to his Brothers & Sisters.

Harriett, eldest daughter of Thomas & Harriett. In 1906 resided with her brother William being a Maiden Lady.

Kate, was married about 1876-7 to Mr Raven, Secretary of Greenwich College.

Ellen, another sister of Harriett – was married to Mr John Binney, brother to Mr C. H. Binney late of Ilford.

Mary, youngest sister – was single in 1900.

Family of Edward Glenny. [Page 466]

Edward Glenny[245] – Uncle to William Wallis Glenny & Brother to Thomas (1861). He was a Market Gardener & built Byfrons about 1850, where he resided until his death in about 1881. He was a member of the Open Brethren & built the chapel in Axe Street for them. He left two sons Edward & Samuel.

Edward, son of above, preacher & member of the Open Brethren. He appears to have managed most of his fathers affairs up to the latters death. After his

---

244 Benjamin Wallis Glenny, wharfinger, contractor, timber, coal, stone, lime, cement, brick, tile & pipe merchant; goods shipped, landed, warehoused & carted; saw mills, Town Quay Steam wharf. (Kelly's 1890).

245 Edward Glenny (1800-1881). Bull Street. (Pigot 1839).

MR FROGLEY'S BARKING: A FIRST SELECTION

fathers death – some years after – he gave up farming – selling most of his land for building purposes & it is called the Gascoigne Estate - & went to reside in Linton Road, where he became Secretary to the Foreign Mission Society. He is also owner of several properties in the town. In 1902 he went to reside at Southend, but now (1911) resides in the district of Manor Park. He has several times travelled abroad as a Missionary but did not stay long. 1887-9 member of the Local Board & 1888 of the Library Committee. Now (1911) living.

Samuel Glenny (Brother of Edward). He was married to Miss Gosling, daughter of Mr Daniel Gosling[246], late of the Swan Inn Barking. He was also brought up to farming but unlike his brother Edward took little interest in Religious matters. The following Epitome will give some idea of his ambitions & various interests. He died at Westcliff August 1910, where he went to reside in 1902. He is buried in the Borough of Southend Cemetery. Born at Barking.

1861	Joined the Volunteers as Private
1862	Made Corporal
1863	Serjeant
1865	Ensign
1869	Went to Australia
1880	Returned to England & rejoind as 1st Lieutenant
1880	Made Captain
1882	Elected a Member of new Local Board & retired in 1887 (of which he was a promoter)
1882	Elected a Guardian of Romford
1882	Agitated for a footpath to Beckton
1888	Appointed Overseer under the new Parish (after the Separation)
1889	Elected a School Board Member & continued so for 10 years
1886	Elected on the Burial Board & continued so 3 years
1892	Became an Auctioneer & his first sale was the effects of Mrs Moffatt – deceased – of Longbridge Road, Barking. His office was on the corner of Cambridge Road & East Street.

---

246 Daniel Gosling died 1884. *St Margaret's churchyard: register of graves.* 1930. p.21.

MR FROGLEY'S BARKING: A FIRST SELECTION

1894	Finally retired from Volunteers as "Honorary Major"
1887 to 1889	Overseer of the Parish, during which time the Parish was divided.
1890	Elected Vestry Clerk at £100 per annum.
1897	Candidate for District Council but defeated
1902	Went to reside at Westcliff, Southend, leaving his sons to manage his business.
1907	Resigned Vestry Clerkship.
1910	Died at Westcliff.

Linton-Road. [Page 376]

Sometimes called Station-Road it is a continuation of Manor Road to East Street & was kerbed & metalled by the Local Board in 1885.

The Standard Beer-house – corner of Kings Road – a few years ago was kept by a Mr William Bailey[247] (who previously had the Prince Albert in Axe Street, now closed). In addition to beer he sold Grocery – in fact with the exception of a tap-room it resembled more of a general shop. In December 1887 he sold it to Mr Copeland - a retired Credit draper – for £1540 freehold who in 1888 dispensed with the Grocery trade & made extensive alterations at a cost of £500. An aged relative & his wife managed it, but not satisfactory to Mr Copeland, hence the old couple went to the Romford Union. In June 1889 a Mr Collins[248] purchased it & he dying in 1890, his widow continued the business. Adjoining the Standard was a large peice of Market Garden land & this Mr Copeland purchased in 1889 for £505 and it is now built upon. It measured 90 feet by 240 feet deep.

William Street, George Street, James Street. Three modern streets made by Mr George Bosworth[249] of the Red Lion from land that was attached to that house. George Street is fully described under North Street & that generally applies to all three. It was in 1898 – after the rebuilding of the Red Lion - that George Street was extended to North Street.

---

247 William Bailey, beerhouse. (White 1863); grocer & beer retailer, Linton Road. (Kelly's 1886).
248 James Collins, beer retailer, Linton Road. (Kelly's 1890).
249 George Bosworth, Red Lion P.H., 66 North Street. (Kelly's 1900).

Page 378 in the manuscript. (See page 55)

The junction of North Street and Barking Broadway, with the Bull on the right. (see page 33).

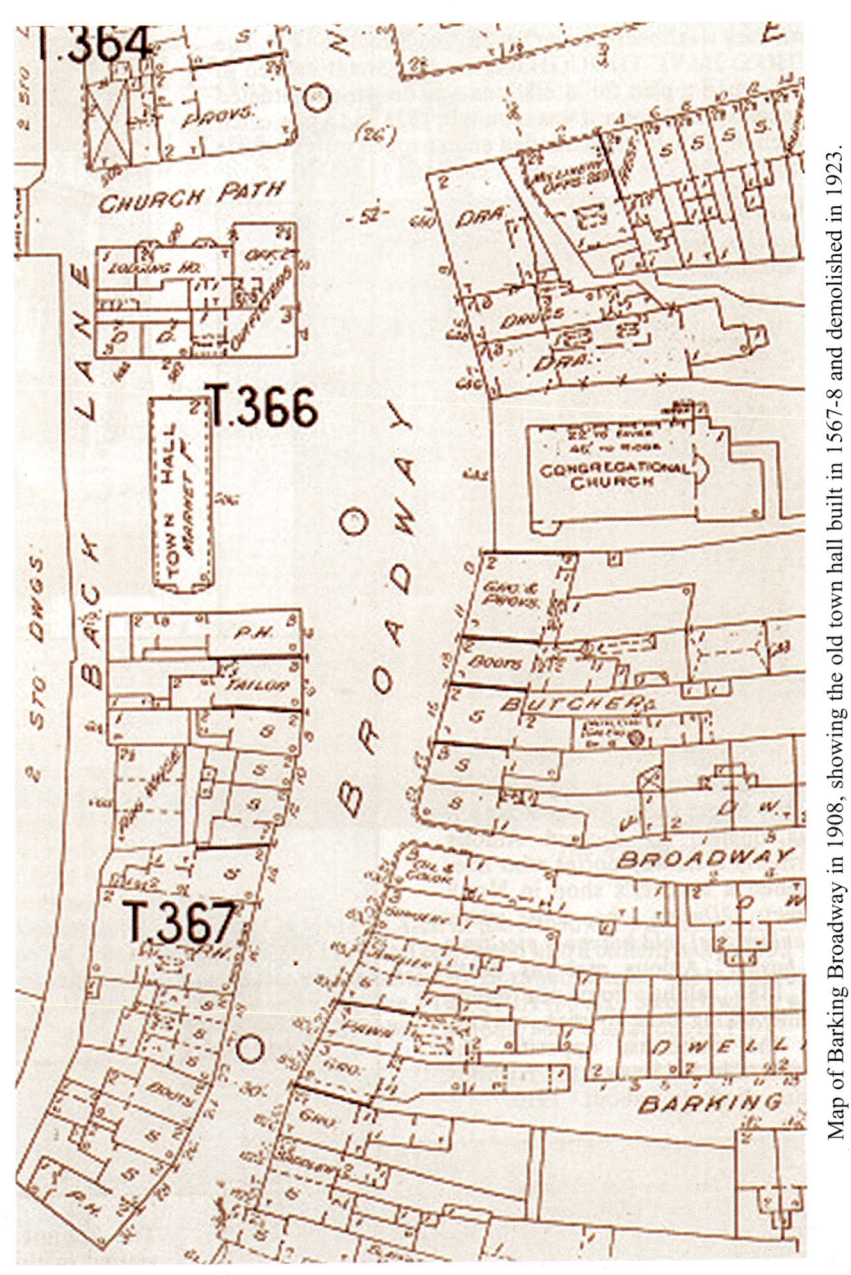

Map of Barking Broadway in 1908, showing the old town hall built in 1567-8 and demolished in 1923. This area was cleared in the 1930s, and Back Lane ceased to exist.

Heath Street in the 1860s, with the entrance to Hart Street on the right. 'Hockley's drapery is in the centre. (see page 62)

Barking Watermill in 1922. (See page 102).

141

Essex Times
13 Mar. 1875

BARKING FAIR.

ANNOUNCEMENT OF SALE.

MR. J. HOLMES

WILL hold his NINTH ANNUAL SALE, at Barking, on Friday, October 22nd, 1875 (in commemoration of Lord Holland, who departed this life October 22nd, 1840), for the SALE of LIVE & DEAD STOCK, and returns his sincere thanks to his numerous Friends and Patrons for the support he has received; and he also wishes to know if any of his supporters have a wish to Abolish the Annual Fair, which he has enjoyed over 50 years. If they have not he hopes they will sign the Petition for its continuance. He also would like to know by whom, or on whose authority, they have dared to attempt to abolish that which has given so much pleasure to the real inhabitants, born in the Town—thorough breds—not those who have come among us without being invited, many of whom think they are somebody, but in the opinion of the " Old uns " are considered Jack Straws, and in some cases a nuisance. My consent has never been asked, and any person or persons so committing themselves for the future will have notice to quit.

JAMES HOLMES.

N.B.—Those who wish to reply must sign their names.

The Petition lies at the George Inn for Signature. It has to be sent to the Secretary of State, on Monday next. All respectable persons are invited to sign it, and any person professing that which they do not possess, wishing to sign, will be shewn the shortest way out.

By order of the Celebrated Jimmy.

(See pages 50-51).

Essex Times Sat. 22 Nov 1873

BARKING FAIR.

A PETITION, is now to be SIGNED at the George Inn, Barking, for the CONTINUANCE OF THE FAIR, so that the old and young may have a little recreation once a year in the old town where they were born; all new comers if they do not like it, let them leave it.

By order,
J. HOLMES.

(See pages 50-51)

J.W. Garland's shop in about 1902. Note the roof garden!
(see footnote 227, page 125).

143

The Barking workhouse building in North Street, by Alfred Bennett Bamford (1905). It was demolished in 1936. (see pages 29-32).

MR FROGLEY'S BARKING: A FIRST SELECTION

Brewery Tap & Brewery - the property of Thomas Wallis Glenny – who originally commenced this business in partnership with his brother George, but George being very religious left the business & entered the Medical profession. I never knew him to have been in practice as he became a Missionary & preached in Africa[250] for many years before his death. The Tap house was formerly opposite to the present one & is now used as a store. The present tap house – a moderate sized bricked building - was built in 1897 & the Licence transferred from the old to the new building. Although a quiet & well conducted business the Temperance party campaigned strenuously opposite the new house. Mr W. W. Glenny who resided at the Paddock, left the town a few years ago & his nephew is I believe manager. He has no children.

Opposite the Catholic Church is 5 newly built houses, the site of which was a good flower garden, occupied by an old couple named Elmore[251] – they lived in a large caravan, which they had built in 1868. After the latter was sold the Caravan was removed to a field – corner of New Street & Bamford Place, but I have not seen it since.

Barking Garden Estate. The frontage of this Estate was from the Brewery to Cambridge Road & extended to the railway. The only Road is Cambridge Road. Previous to 1879 Cambridge Road only had a few houses in it & from the top of it was a path leading to Linton Road. This path was afterwards made into a road - an extension of Cambridge Road. Formerly Copyhold it was converted into Freehold in 1854.

The modern house at the corner of James Street was built by Mrs Ringer, a former landlady of the Still, Fisher Street. For many years it was occupied – after her death – by Mr Stanley Preston[252], Solicitor of Stratford, but now (1912) the tenant is Mr W. Chalk[253] – recently retired from the Railway. William Chalk, late Stationmaster at Barking, retired in Sept 1912. In 1854 his father was appointed the 1st Station Master here & he dying in 1875 was succeeded by his son Albert[254] & who in 1892 was appointed Station Master

---

250 North Africa Mission (Edward H. Glenny, Hon. Sec.), 19, 21, 23, 29 & 31 Linton Road. (Kelly's 1900).

251 East of London Family History Society: *1851 census index series: vol.1, pt.4: Barking.* 1984. p.12.

252 Stanley R. Preston, solicitor, 4 Cambridge Road. (Kelly's 1890); 17 Linton Road. (Kelly's1895); solicitor & commissioner for oaths, 17 Linton Road. (Kelly's 1900).

253 William Chalk, station master, East Street. (Kelly's 1900).

254 Albert Chalk, station master, East Street. (Kelly's 1890).

MR FROGLEY'S BARKING: A FIRST SELECTION

at Southend, when William, his brother, who previously was Station master at Plaistow & later took the Lord Raglan, & failed there, returned to the Railway & was appointed at Barking in 1892.

Dove-House Estate. [Pages 469-476]

This Estate – also called Malmaynes[255] – was situated at the North of the Town and what it comprised will be best understood by reference to the two plans annexed – one plan as it was in the year 1800, and the other plan as it was in 1900.

No.1 Plan. As it was in the year 1800.

No.1. This comprised 299 perches, and on it was a building used as a beerhouse and stables. The Quakers had also held meetings there.

No.2 and 7. Roding Lodge and garden, containing 1 acre and 6 perches. In 1827 it was tenanted by a William Palmer, farmer, and owned by Mr John C. Joyner. The old house was a fine square bricked building and was erected about 1809 on the site of a smaller one, which then belonged to Mr George Spurrell, Farmer, JP, and who farmed all this land until he disposed of it[256]. Other later tenants was the Rev. Mr. Corby, Congregational Minister, Mr Robert Hickes in 1855 & Mr Edward Sage, an antiquarian and Steward to the Lord of the Manor[257]. He in late years resided at Stoke Newington. Mr Brady, Solicitor of London, and during his residence this house was destroyed by

---

255 William Holmes Frogley's most successful venture into original research is contained in his account of the Dove House Estate, which most probably derives from a descent of title contained in the deeds of the property. Frogley positively identifies fields of the Malmaynes estate as lying in Barking town, information which would have been of crucial importance to the authors of *VCH Essex*, vol.5, if the manuscript had been available. Bert Lockwood strongly suspects that Frogley found a copy of the complex descent of title in the deeds of property held by his father. Joseph Frogley built Laurel Cottage in Queens Road, tenanted Ivy Cottage next door and owned the freehold of cottages in Manor Road – all of which were built on sections of the Dove House Estate auctioned in 1850. Young William Holmes Frogley must have been brought up in Ivy Cottage – might it be too fanciful to suppose that sight of these deeds and plans may have helped to stimulate his interest in local history?

256 The surrender of George Spurrell and Elizabeth his wife to John Joyner at a Court Baron for the Manor of Barking on 21st October 1809 can be found in the appropriate Court minutes and Court book at Essex Record Office (D/DHs M19, fo.5 etc & M21 fo.5 etc.).

257 Edward Sage (1807-1864) described himself as Steward in 1854. He was, in fact, Deputy Steward for over 35 years. His son Edward John (d.1904) added to his extensive collection of material relating to Barking and Dagenham, which was left to Stoke Newington Library and later transferred to Essex Record Office in 1946.

MR FROGLEY'S BARKING: A FIRST SELECTION

fire in 1868 – the only portion saved was that part containing the front entrance door, and it still stands. The house was rebuilt and became the residence of Robert Hewett Esq of Smack owning fame. Retiring from business he removed to Bromley, Kent, and his son Robert is the present owner and occupier. (For Hewett family see Fishery).

No.3. Probably the site of the Dove-House (or Cote) and it contained 1 acre 2 rods 9 perches. This peice of land is now bounded by Kings Road, Queens Road, Manor Road and North Street.

No.4 and 6. These two peices of land contained (No.4) 1 acre 12 perches and (No.6) 6 acres 3 rods 13 perches and in the admission to the Rolls of the Manor of Barking is called Malmaynes[258]. On No.4 is the North Street Schools, and on No.6 is a footpath to the Ilford Lane from a lane – now Queens Road.

No.2 Plan – representing the year 1900.

The above very rough plan shews the roads on the Estate at the present time, but I am certain that a few centuries back this estate formed a portion of one of the most important Estates in Barking. The fact of it possessing a Dove Cote is sufficient to prove its importance. There was only one house possessed a Dove-Cote in Barking besides this and that was Jenkins, and this Manor of Malmaynes was amalgamated with Jenkins. This comparative small portion of this Estate - comprised in Plans – was in 1745 the property of Sir Chris[259] Gascoyne of Byfrons, and in that year, and in consideration of the sum of £200 paid by Mr George Spurrell, the former leased to the latter all the land shown on the Plan. Roding Lodge was then occupied by a Mr Edward Bullinger. Mr Spurrell died in 1769 and his son Joseph also died in 1779, being succeded by his son George Spurrell JP and a Director of the old Workhouse. This Mr Spurrell appears to have got himself financially entangled, and caused him to loose this Estate. The following is the facts:-

"Thomas Pittman Esqr of Loxford, a celebrated Essex Farmer, died in 1791, and he bequeathed his Estate to his children – Thomas, John, Charles and Elizabeth – in trust, appointing Mr George Spurrell of Roding Lodge, Mr Whitmore of London, John Tylor of Romford and Thomas Newman of Eastbury House. Mr Newman married the daughter Elizabeth. It appears that

---

258 It was only possible to verify this statement when the Barking manorial records were deposited in the Essex Record Office at the end of 1968.

259 Should be Crisp.

MR FROGLEY'S BARKING: A FIRST SELECTION

Mr Spurrell took upon himself the sole management of the late Mr Pittmans Estate, and that he used the money for his own purposes, instead of applying it as the Will directed. Subsequently an Action in Chancery was brought against the Executors – Except Thomas Newman who previously died. No answer was put in by them, but Mr Spurrell claimed compensation for managing the Farm Books &c and later the case came before referees, who decided against Mr Spurrell, and after some deductions ordered Mr Spurrell the sum of £3528 to Mr Sterry, Solicitor of Romford who acted for the four Legatees. Being unable to comply with this order, he secured his interest in this Estate and other properties owned by him in Barking. This new Trust was handed over to Mr Sterry and another, with powers to sell if Mr Spurrell failed to pay the amount in three years, at the same time he remained in possession and Interest ran on the amount. The Security comprised 10 acres of arable, 5 acres of meadow, 5 of Marsh, a house and large garden, and the Trust was dated 1804. It was however discovered that a large amount was due to Mr Spurrell and which was not mentioned when the Award was made, so it was agreed too by all to accept the sum of £3000 in full discharge, and which sum Mr Joseph Cuff, of Movers Farm Barking, advanced in 1805, upon Mortgage for 2 years at £400 Interest. At the end of that time Mr Spurrell sold all of it to John Joyner Esqr of London (in 1808) for the sum of £4750 - of which £3998 was due to Mr Cuff. John Cuthbert Joyner – subject to an Annuity of £400 to be paid to his wife Betsy. She died in 1835. Mr John Cuthbert Joyner and Mary his wife, in 1847 disposed of the same to Samuel Bamford Esqre of Brixton, and the roads being made, the land was sold by portions in 1850 by Auction".

Queens Road – it was only a pathway and was evidently made just after 1847. In this road is the Reservoir, erected by the Water Company for the supply of the town. From this Reservoir is [ ] modern villas, built by Mr Edward Fitt, Chemist[260]. The site of these Villas was a well kepted garden and orchard, belonging to Mr Daniel Hawes, Farmer. He resided in one of the Villas – opposite the "Swan". The land he farmed is now the Recreation Ground, Longbridge Road. Mr Hawes later went to reside in Hawthorn Terrace, Ripple Road[261], which he built and where he died, his widow subsequently marrying Mr Chalk, the Station Master at Barking.

260 Edward Fitt died 1880. "Eight years Churchwarden of this Parish". *St Margaret's churchyard: register of graves*. 1930. p.208.
261 Daniel Hawes, 8 Hawthorn Terrace. (Kelly's 1874). Died 1875.

MR FROGLEY'S BARKING: A FIRST SELECTION

Laurel Cottage, [Page 472]

built in [ ] by Mr Joseph Frogley[262] as a private residence and was occupied by Mr Todd, who came to Barking to superintend the construction of a Sewer near Creeksmouth but the project failed, and for many years the brick tunnel began to go into ruins. Mr Todd left Barking, and the house was taken by Mr Daniel Gosling. (Daniel Gosling was a Smith by trade and during the "Fishery" time, he carried on his business at the rear of the Fishing Smack, Fisher Street. Later he for many years had a general shop at the corner of Nelson Street. Removing to Laurel Cottage, his eldest daughter continued in the shop until she married Mr Samuel Glenny. After retiring from the Swan, Mr Gosling purchased the Villa opposite, and resided there until his death in 1884 and his widow[263] died there in [ ]. Their children, all of whom was married, sold the Freehold of the Swan in 1892-3).

In 1871, shortly after taking the house on a 21 years lease at a Rental of £18 a year, he [Mr Gosling] obtained a Licence to sell beer on the premises and on the opening night he gave all the beer free. Mr Gosling was very doubtful as to the sign of the house, Some suggesting "the Goose" but eventually he named it the Swan. (The sign of the "Swan" is very common in Essex, and singularly this bird is very fond of liquids ...). He was very successful, and in 1882 purchased the Freehold for £500 and soon after retired. He then made a good stroke of business as he sold the Business only for £600 to a Mr J. Curtis, a foreman at Beckton Gas Works, and raised the rent to £40 a year. Mr Joseph Curtis, however, who had a large family, eloped with another woman, and since then the house often changed hands. The house was finally closed in 1906 – the Licence being surrendered in favor of another house at Ilford. The house was divided into two – one a private house and the corner a shop.

Queens Road was made up by the old Urban Authority, but it was kerbed and metalled in 1885 by the Local Board.

Roding Cottages (four) is built on the site of a farm yard, and Mr Samuel Baxter resided in the cottage.

---

262 The author's father Joseph Frogley (1819-1902). The 1881 census shows Joseph Frogley, then a watchman at Beckton Gas Works, his wife Jane, and two of their sons, Joseph and Charles, living in Queens Road in the house next to the Swan beerhouse (Laurel Cottage). He was living in Windsor Cottage, Longbridge Road, in 1890 and at 44 Longbridge Road in 1895 and 1900. (Kelly's).

263 Mrs Gosling, 13 Queen's Road. (Kelly's 1890).

MR FROGLEY'S BARKING: A FIRST SELECTION

Kings Road, [Page 474]

originally "Love Lane", was made about 185? but the portion from Manor Road to the Railway was previous to 1856 called "Plough lane". It is composed of cottages with wooden fences in front, but these are gradually dissappearing. In this road lived several captains of fishing vessels. Also here Mr Kirkman – formerly a traveller for the Barking Brewery - commenced the business of a cow-keeper[264]. It is now Kirkman and Sons, at various addresses. In this road also was some market gardeners, who had their yards and outbuildings, but they have also gone. Here also is a small bakers shop, which once did a very thriving trade. Mr J. Johnson[265], Baker of East Street, commenced business here in this shop.

Manor Road. This road, in common with Kings Road and Queens Road, was a small lane, and all these lanes was bounded by hedges. In Manor Road the Holly bush predominated – hence Holly Cottages. At one corner is a General shop, kept by Miss Esther Gibbard[266], and it had a Licence attached to it. The sign of the house was the "Holly Bush". The terrace adjoining is also her property. The owner at the time was a Mr Mark Gibbard, widower, and he resided there with his daughter Esther Ann Gibbard. He also introduced the coal trade, and built the shed in the rear.

The Forresters. This Beerhouse was situated at the corner of Kings Road and Manor Road – opposite the "Holly Bush". Previously a cottage when the licence was obtained, and afterwards the adjoining cottage was added for a tap-room. The tenant for many years – named Freeman – occassionally had some sports held in the roadway, such as climbing the greasy pole &c. He died about 1868 and his widow subsequently married a Mr Carter[267] who held these sports annually. The house was closed in 1902 as a surrender for the Westbury Arms, and the house was purchased by Mr Copeland, and it is now (1908) a Greengrocers.

---

264 Benjamin Kirkman, cowkeeper, King's Road. (Kelly's 1886).
265 James Johnson, baker, 26 East Street. (Kelly's 1890, 1900).
266 Frederick Lewis Gibbard, grocer, North Street. (Pigot 1839). Mrs Esther Gibbard, shopkeeper, 53 Linton Road. (Kelly's 1890), 61 Linton Road. (Kelly's 1900); Miss Esther Gibbard, shopkeeper, 61 Linton Road. (Kelly's 1894); Mrs Esther A. Gibbard, grocer & beer retailer, Manor Road. (Kelly's 1874). Gibbard entries in *St Margaret's churchyard: register of graves*. 1930. p.199-200.
267 George Carter, beer retailer, Manor Road. (Kelly's 1874).

MR FROGLEY'S BARKING: A FIRST SELECTION

Church Road. **[Page 475]**

This road was probably the first road made on the Estate, and contained at least one resident in 1845. In 1887 the Local Board sewered and made up this road. In this road the residents generally consisted of retired tradesmen but its appearance was very much altered by the recent railway extension.

The Brittannia. A common and a Geographical sign. The old house was a square, bricked, double fronted one, and entered by three steps, with bay-windows on each side. On the left of the doorway was the Bar and on the left the tap-room. In 1868[268] the tenant was a Mr Lewis, and he was succeeded by Mr McAlister of Creeksmouth[269], and during his time the house was nearly rebuilt, but not made larger. He died there in 1881, and the same year the Freehold was sold by Auction. The next tenant was Mr Williams Evans [270], of the "Victoria", Plaistow. He died here in 1886 and shortly after his widow sold the business to Mr Kitson (in 1887)[271]. In 1898 he made great alterations in the house, and had removed the old Sign-Post that stood on the edge of the path for so many years. Mr Kitson was born at Hadleigh, in Norfolk, and he died 3rd February 1906 while on a visit to Hastings, leaving – provided for – a wife & 7 children viz:- Harry: Frank: Herbert: George: Jenny: Agnes and Ethel.

Victoria Gardens – situate in Queens Road – is a Triangular peice of land – formerly used as Market garden. Originally a pathway crossed it from Queens Road to Church Road, but the Railway divided it & in 1894 it was sold by an Order of the Chancery Court, by Mr S. Glenny to the School Board, who again in 1895 sold it to the Council. It is about three quarters of an Acre in Extent. The Unemployed were at once placed on it to get it in order, as it was decided to convert it into a public garden – the gardens is beautifully laid out.

New Street **[Page 476]**

– formerly occupied by an inferior class of people, and thus it was always known as "Rotten-Row". The name New Street was only given to it in recent years, and I believe that this street is the only improvement made to any thoroughfare by the so-called recent Railway improvement.

Bamford Place. A small thoroughfare now mostly wiped out by the Railway

---

268 Benjamin Shepherd is listed in 1863 (White).
269 Alexander MacAlister, Britannia, Church Road. (Kelly's 1874).
270 Thomas Evans, Britannia P.H., Church Road. (Kelly's 1886).
271 Walter John Kitson, Britannia P.H., Church Road. (Kelly's 1890).

extension. Its residents were mostly men employed on the Railway. It was in continuation of Kings Road (the railway dividing) and it took its name from Mr Bamford, who purchased this Estate. On one corner the Earl of Beaconsfield stood. It obtained its Licence in 1883 by a John Moore and the house previously was Wakering House. It later changed hands to Mr J. Sills [272], but in 1906 it was pulled down with about 20 cottages by the Railway Company.

Tanner Street. [Pages 477-480]

Tanner Street, probably named after some family who may have resided there[273], connects North Street with Ilford Lane, and therefore is very ancient only as a lane. It was tar-paved in 1889, but in consequence of the recent so called railway improvements.

Northbury House. There are two "Northbury Houses" in Barking but this one is a modern house, standing in its own grounds at the corner of Harts Lane. It is brick built and slated, double-fronted. The Marchant family resided here many years[274]. They were smackowners in the town. James Marchant died in 1811, and his son Henry – a devoted Wesleyan – died here in 1882. Also died here his wife Susan, and their only daughter. Later Mr J. Braund removed here from East-Ham[275], as he being connected with the Socialistic party, was very active in the town at elections, being a member of the Town-Council, the School-Board and Burial Board. He did not remain here so very long, and Mr Davies[276] has resided there since. He is Manager of the Malt House at Barking – Churchwarden – and has served upon most of the local bodies.

Adjoining is some old wooden cottages – and we come to The Haunted House

---

272 Jabez Sills, ironmonger & beer retailer, 34 & 36 New Street. (Kelly's 1890, 1894, 1900).
273 It is surprising that it did not occur to Frogley that the name might have been connected with the tanner's craft. See footnote 274.
274 The Northbury House in which the Marchants resided stood on the corner of Harts Lane and Tanner Street, looking down North Street. Up to the mid-19th century this was the site of Tanners Farm where Nicholas Mead, tanner, dwelt in 1669. In the 19th century there was a third Northbury House down Hart Street. The smackowner Christopher Spashett (Pigot 1839) lived there and later Edward Steane, soap manufacturer (White 1848).
275 See: Lockwood, Herbet Hope *Barking 100 years ago*. Privately published by the author, 1990, page 29 onwards. John Wilton Braund is listed at The Germans, North Street, in 1890 (Kelly's).
276 Edward A. Davies, Northbury House, Tanner Street. (Kelly's 1890).

MR FROGLEY'S BARKING: A FIRST SELECTION

– an old red bricked house, but why it was said to be haunted I do not know[277].

J. Louth Esq.[278] Adjoining – and before crossing the railway - was a high, but heavy built brick house, nearly square with a good garden – probably the oldest in this street. Mr Joseph Louth, the general manager of the London & Tilbury Railway resided there as soon as the railway came. He lived here in 1860, and died there in [ ]. The house was demolished in December 1906.

The Railway Crossing here had gates, and a small dwelling for the gate-keeper, but all this has gone since 1906 and the roadway divided by brick walls. More will be said of these crossings under "Railway". The railway extension also caused some cottages to be pulled down, and also a fine red bricked modern house – Chesnut House – for many years the residence of Mr G. A. Burrell, and later by Mr James Morgan (see East Street).

Chesnut House, [Page 479]

so named from a large Chesnut tree that stood in the garden at the side of the house, and it over-lapped the street. This House was demolished in 1897[279], as the Railway took this property previously for an extension at that time and the Company in 1895 erected a footbridge, but in 1907 additional lines was laid down and the present foot-bridge erected. The site of Chesnut House is now Victoria Road, and which was made in 1897 – the year of her late Majesties Diamond Jubilee. Opposite was one of the town-pumps.

Vine-Cottage – now gradually becoming delapidated - was the old police station – when there was only two officers in the town. The Metropolitan Police supplanted these. The Rev G. Corney – an old Congregational Minister - resided here for a time. In 1868 a family named Collier lived at Vine Cottage. Mr Collier possessed "Collier Row", a row of cottages in

---

277 The naturalist Sir Alfred Russel Wallace (1823-1913) lived in an old cottage, Holly Lodge, in Tanner Street. He is listed there in the 1871 census. "Wallace became converted to Spiritualism in 1866 and we know that he was attending seances while living in Barking, and may even have held them in his house at Barking. Wallace was certainly holding seances in his house at Grays a year or two later. This may possibly explain why Holly House was known as the haunted house". Information from Bill George, *Barking & District Historical Society newsletter*, May 2001,p.2-4.

278 Joseph Louth, railway superintendent. (White 1848); The Bays, Tanner Street. (Kelly's 1886); 23 Tanner Street. (Kelly's 1895). Died 1902. *St Margaret's churchyard: register of graves*. 1930. p.191.

279 Mrs Willet was at Chestnut House, Tanner Street, in 1890. (Kelly's).

MR FROGLEY'S BARKING: A FIRST SELECTION

Fisher Street. He was an Artist and at that time all the Licenced houses in the Town possessed pictures painted by him of the Barking Fleet in the North Sea. His son William Collier married Jane, a daughter of the late Daniel Gosling[280] of the "Swan" beer-house, Queens Road. He is an house painter and was recently living at Southend. Of more recent times Mr Joseph Liall resided and died there. He with his brother Mark, commenced business as the familiar rag & bone dealers &c and both of them an old inhabitant informed me travelled the town daily buying these things, and they were very successful. Some years later Joseph became a large dealer in all kinds of metal, and he purchased the old and historical Brass candle chandliers that hung suspended from the ceiling of the Parish Church. The Rev Mr Bloomfield, Vicar sold them to him as old Brass, but Mr Liall resold them (as he told me himself) to a gentleman for his mansion in London.

Dolbys Farm. Opposite Church Road was two low built brick houses, laying some 80 feet from the street, with barns and other outbuildings. The last tenants was a family – two brothers – named Dolby[281]. Farm Cottages Nos 71-73 is now built on this site. The aspect of this street has so changed during the past few years that a resident of 30 years ago would scarcely recognise it, and as regards the "improvements" it is all on the side of the railway – certainly not in its appearance. The blocking of an ancient roadway appears to me monstrous – but I suppose in this case it could not be avoided.

Creeksmouth. [Pages 493-496]

This isolated hamlet of Barking – seldom visited by ordinary visitors or noticed by historians is situated at the mouth of the River Roding – at the spot where it flows into the Thames. Originally this spot was selected by the government as a convenient place to build a Magazine for gunpowder, as in the year 1719 the magistrates at Quarter Sessions selected a peice of land here for the storage of Gunpowder, & after the magazine was built, it was undoubtedly the first building erected on this spot & according to the Parish Registers was assessed for some years to Barking Parish at £20 per annum.

I have not traced when it was transferred from government property to private ownership, but evidently the government owned it some 50 years. In

---

280 Daniel Gosling, beer retailer, Queen's Road. (Kelly's 1874). East of London Family History Society: *1851 census index series: vol.1, pt.4: Barking.* 1984. p.15-16.

281 Benjamin Dolby, market gardener, Tanner Street. (Kelly's 1874).

MR FROGLEY'S BARKING: A FIRST SELECTION

1876 they belonged to a Mr Sharp & in 1881 a Mr Westfield possessed them & he in 1885 disposed of them to the Chilworth Gunpowder Company[282], which was incorporated & a certificate given to them. I am informed that upwards of 100 tons of Gunpowder have been stored in these Magazines at one time. In consequence of factories & dwelling house being erected near to them, they were considered dangerous & a nuisance, hence in 1888 the Barking Local Board unsuccessively applied to the Courts to have this nuisance abated.

It was however the various factories that have been erected at this spot, that accounts for a village coming into existence. In 1858 the late Sir J. B. Lawes of Rothamsted, Herts[283] – in conjunction with Messrs F. S. Hempleman & Co & Mr William Harvey founded & established the Chemical works here, & subsequently dwelling houses were built for the workmen. During 1887-8 extensive alterations was carried out at these works with a view to reducing to the lowest possible point the cost of Production. The Acid plant was re-constructed by the erection of 6 new chambers to replace the last remaining six of the old plant & by which 22,000 tons of required Acid could then be produced per annum. In 1889 it was stated that the Company could financially be compared favorably with any institution of a similar kind in the Country.

In 1893 about 400 men was engaged at the Works. A fire occurred here in November 1893 – destroying several thousands of pounds worth of Property. That part known as the New Mills was destroyed with the valuable plant & other contents – the buildings being about 140 feet x 150 feet. No workman was thrown idle, in consequence of the lack of the Manager – Mr McAlister [284] (died April 1896) – who diverted the firms engines to that part facing the Thames & which were in close proximity to the Acid Tanks – saving the destruction of the whole factory. In September 1889 – following a strike, there was a general lock-out of the men – subscriptions amounting to £50 for the 292 families suffering was raised, but it only lasted a few weeks – the works being reopened upon the mens terms.

---

282 "The still-existing private powder-mill at Chilworth, in Surrey, was established in 1570". *VCH Essex*: vol.2. 1907. p.451.
283 Sir John Bennet Lawes (1814-1900).
284 John McAlister, Creek Mouth. (White 1863).

MR FROGLEY'S BARKING: A FIRST SELECTION

Crows Factory[285] [Page 494]

– a short distance East of the above – also a Chemical Factory, was closed in 1898 & the business transferred to Harts Marsh, Barking.

The Village is in close proximity to Lawes Factory. In 1889 there was 55 houses & a population of 250. There is also a Mission Church – called St Pauls Mission Room – Brick built – the services being conducted by a Curate from Barking. There is also an Inn, called the "Crooked Billet" – the Licence is probably older than the Village. Originally it was a small wooden house, at a later date enlarged. Fairs were occassionally here – previous to the Village being built - & was well patronised by the Fishermen of Barking. In 1860 a Mr William Kirk[286] had it & he probably opened it. He was succeeded by a Mr Harry Coates – a fisherman who took it & eventually was able to retire from it & after resided at Barking[287]. He died March 1894 Aged 88 leaving his son well provided for & who also resides at Barking. There was also the village constable – P.C. Gatwood – who joining the Metropolitan Force in 1865 was in 1870 transferred to Creeksmouth & remained there until his retirement upon his pension in 1891 (November).

On September 3rd 1878 was the evening of the terrible disaster to the Princess Alice, when over 800 persons was drowned off Barking Reach. A Village fete was being held that day & amidst their pleasure, the villagers heard the screams – left the field & rendered what help they could to the victims – a day not to be forgot by them[288].

In August 1891 a bottle nosed Whale was captured here 25 feet long & 18 feet in girth. It was first seen by a bargeman who with others killed it & brought it ashore near the Magazines & where it was exhibited – hundreds paying 6 pence each to view it.

---

285 Crow, Thomas & Sons, manufacturers of creosote, tar, pitch, marine engine & cylinder oils etc, Harts Lane. (Kelly's 1900).

286 George Strutt, sluice keeper to Mr William Kirk, Rippleside. (Kelly's 1890).

287 Possibly Henry Coates, 18 Cambridge Road. (Kelly's 1890).

288 "Even strong swimmers were sucked down or choked by the swirling filth. Most bodies were never found, and the accident remains Britain's worst inshore shipping disaster". *Old Ordnance Survey maps: London sheet 68: Creekmouth 1894.* 1988.

MR FROGLEY'S BARKING: A FIRST SELECTION

The writer well remembers [Page 495]

the difficulty in walking from the town to Creeksmouth village. One would have to walk along the zigzag bank of the Roding – no lights - & a path about 3 feet in width. In foggy, wet or dark nights it was dangerous. But for many years the majority of the work-people was compelled to use this path. Tradespeople usually conveyed their goods by means of rowing boats from the Creek. During 1887 an agitation was started to construct a foot-path accross the marshes in as near a straight line as possible, as by this time several other factories had sprung up between Creeksmouth & Barking. It was in 1888 – by the assistance of the Factory owners, tradesmen & others - that subscriptions were raised and a Foot-path – 15 feet wide – was made, costing upwards of £700 & lighted with oil-lamps. This was a great boon to the workman. Later about 1893 a carriage road was constructed, the various landowners giving the land occupied by the roadway.

This carriage road was decided to be made by the Barking Town Council & in December 1894 – there being no lamps on it – the inhabitants of Creeksmouth petitioned the Council for some, but the Council declined unless they (the inhabitants) erected a lamp post at their own costs. In August 1895 the Council commenced the new carriage way & in doing so they broke up an old brick culvert near a factory called Davys[289] & fenced the road. (The old Brick Culvert was originally a brick tunnel – about 5 feet in diameter – built for a sewer in 1868. It was never finished but left to gradually fall into ruins. The Manager or Foreman who superintended the building of this old sewer was a Mr Todd, who resided at Laurel Cottage (afterwards the Swan) Queens Road, Barking. When the building of the sewer stoped he left the town). In 1897 the Council erected Lamps & have since controlled & lighted the road. Upwards of £1100 was expended in laying extra surface drains & laying down Kentish flints &c.

Leaving the Village on the way to Barking the following factories is built :

The Cork Pavement Works. [Page 496]

A destructive fire occurred here in August 1894 & destroyed the works. The damage was estimated at £3000 (see Fisher Street for this Factory).

---

[289] James Davey, tar distiller, Barking Creek. (Kelly's 1874); William Davey, tar & chemical works, Barking Creek. (Kelly's 1900).

MR FROGLEY'S BARKING: A FIRST SELECTION

The Coalite Ltd works. In 1911 the Offices of this Company was removed to 119 Finsbury Pavement E.C. - & at that date the financial position of the Company was not flourishing, although improvements were seen. Also about this time a reorganisation took place, & the undertaking from 1911 (April) would be known as the British Coalite Company. Also at this time the Company had works distributed in other localities & which were unprofitable – viz at Plymouth and Hythe the works was closed up – and the entire operation of the Company was then centred at Barking. At Wednesfield their works was also closed. The working system of the Company was entirely changed by their gradually taking over the distribution of its output direct to the consumer, & under a continuance of the present method of manufacture & business management, the Company can earn 4/- per ton nett on every ton of coal carbonised (Coalite Ltd report for 1910).

Johnstons. Ship Building yard – situated near the Town quay. In 1895 the townspeople were elated to hear the above yard would be established here, but it turned out to be only a dream. A Mr Alexander Johnstone applied to the Council for a piece of land called the "Saltings" as he intended opening an iron & steel barge building yard. The Council decided to let him the Saltings & some adjoining land upon Lease for 21 years at a Peppercorn rent for 1 year: 6 years at £10: 7 at £15 & 7 at £20 per Annum. A Provisional Agreement was signed, but he refused to sign the Lease. The Council spent about £70 upon the site, but enquiries & other circumstances proved Mr Johnstone to be an undesirable tenant & the whole matter collapsed.

MR FROGLEY'S BARKING: A FIRST SELECTION

FURTHER READING.

Clifford, Tony	*Barking and Dagenham buildings past and present.* London Borough of Barking & Dagenham, Libraries Dept, 1992.
Clifford, Tony	*Barking pubs past and present.* London Borough of Barking & Dagenham, Libraries Dept, 1995.
Lockwood, Herbert H.	*"The exposure of Frogley"* in: *Ilford Historical Society newsletter,* no.76, March 2001.
Lockwood, Herbert H.	*"Frogley's manuscript history of Barking"* in: *Cockney Ancestor,* no.66, Spring 1995, p.33-37.
Lockwood, Herbert H.	*"The Frogley MS"* in: *Barking & District Historical Society newsletter,* May 2001.
Lockwood, Herbert H.	*The Frogleys of Barking (main line).* Unpublished genealogy. 1993.
Lockwood, Herbert H.	*An unknown illustrated history of Barking.* Transcript of a lecture given to Barking Historical Society [undated].
Oxley, James Edwin	*Barking and Ilford: an extract from the Victoria History of the County of Essex, Volume 5.* Barking & Dagenham Libraries/Redbridge Libraries, 1987.
Oxley, James Edwin	*Barking vestry minutes and other parish documents.* Benham, 1955.

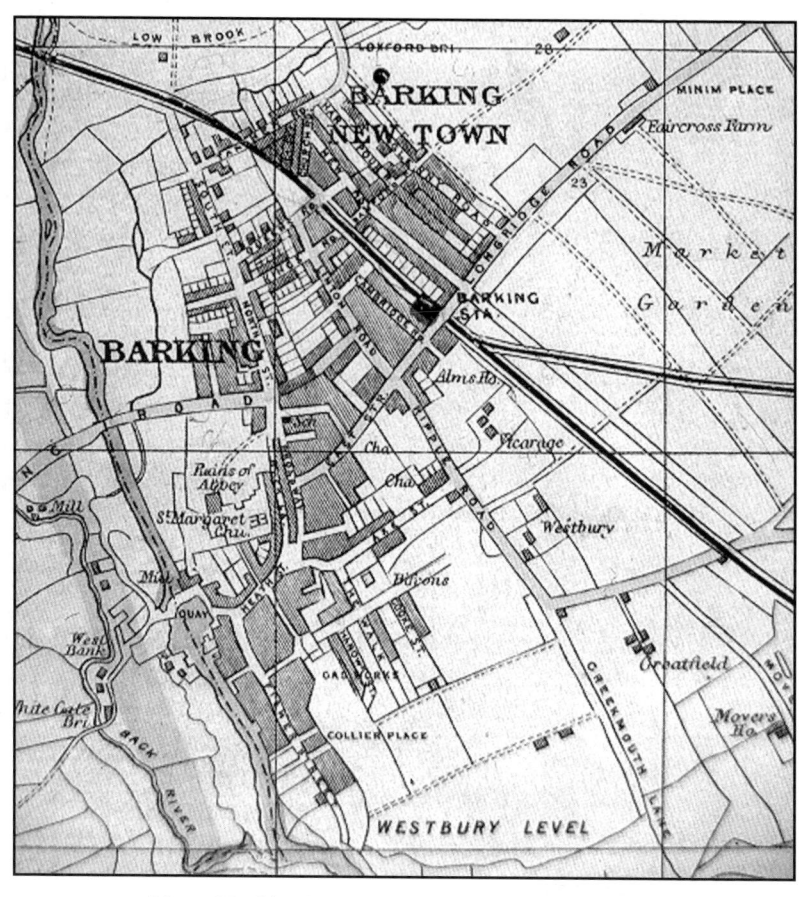

Map of Barking in about 1880 (Philip's Library Atlas).

Cover picture: the Fishing Smack, pre 1902.
(photograph loaned by Mrs Blyth of Upminster)